LOOKS LIKE DAYLIGHT

LOOKS LIKE DAYLIGHT

VOICES OF INDIGENOUS KIDS

DEBORAH ELLIS

Foreword by **Loriene Roy**

Groundwood Books / House of Anansi Press
Toronto   Berkeley

Photo credits: Pages 54 and 56, Alvin John; pages 132 and 133, Liza Holly; page 207, Rachael Waller Photography; page 218, Kara Briggs; pages 41, 83, 91, 97, 117, 118 and 130, courtesy of the children's families. All other photographs courtesy of the author.

Published in Canada and the USA in 2013 by Groundwood Books

Groundwood Books / House of Anansi Press
110 Spadina Avenue, Suite 801, Toronto, Ontario M5V 2K4
or c/o Publishers Group West
1700 Fourth Street, Berkeley, CA 94710

We acknowledge for their financial support of our publishing program the Canada Council for the Arts, the Government of Canada through the Canada Book Fund (CBF) and the Ontario Arts Council.

Canada Council   Conseil des Arts
for the Arts   du Canada

ONTARIO ARTS COUNCIL
CONSEIL DES ARTS DE L'ONTARIO

Library and Archives Canada Cataloguing in Publication
Ellis, Deborah
Looks like daylight : voices of indigenous kids / written
by Deborah Ellis ; foreword by Loriene Roy.
Issued also in electronic format.
ISBN 978-1-55498-120-5
1. Indian children—North America—Juvenile literature.
2. Native children—Canada—Juvenile literature. I. Title.
E98.C5E55 2013   j305.23089'97   C2013-900400-9

Cover photographs: Frames from *Tsu Heidei Shugaxtutaan* ("We will again open this container of wisdom that has been left in our care"), a two-part video by Nicholas Galanin, 2011, www.beatnation.org/nicholas-galanin.html.
Design by Michael Solomon

Groundwood Books is committed to protecting our natural environment. As part of our efforts, the interior of this book is printed on paper that contains 100% post-consumer recycled fibers, is acid-free and is processed chlorine-free.

Printed and bound in Canada

All royalties from the sale of this book will go to the First Nations Child and Family Caring Society of Canada, which supports and advocates for indigenous youth, including those in foster care. Their vision is a generation of First Nations children who have the same opportunities to succeed, celebrate their culture and be proud of who they are as any other children in Canada.

First Nations Child and Family Caring Society
    of Canada
309 Cooper Street, Suite 401
Ottawa, Ontario Canada K2P 0G5
613-230-5885
info@fncaringsociety.com
www.fncaringsociety.com

Think not of yourselves, O Chiefs, nor of your own generation. Think of continuing generations of our families. Think of our grandchildren and of those yet unborn, whose faces are coming from beneath the ground.

— Peacemaker, founder of the Iroquois Confederacy

Foreword

Indigenous peoples are still here, as the stories of these forty-five young people attest. These are the children of the Blackfoot, Choctaw, Cree, Haida Gwaii, Inuit, Lakota, Métis, Nez Perce, Ojibwe, Mi'kmaq, Navajo, Pueblo of Laguna, Pueblo of Santo Domingo, Seminole, and other American Indian and First Nations people. These are also children of mixed or blended heritage. They live in the urban cities of St. Paul, Toronto and Ottawa, on the pueblos of New Mexico, in the Everglades, on the Pine Ridge Reservation, in Nunavut, on traditional homelands, reservations and reserves across Canada and the United States. Their parents or caretakers are close or distant, loving or aloof, known or unknown, admired, acknowledged, forgiven — but not forgotten.

These are the stories of young people who have inherited the challenges of colonialism. These challenges of family dissolution, family/intimate partner violence, diabetes, alcoholism/drug abuse, foster care, bullying, Fetal Alcohol Spectrum Disorder (FASD), self-abuse and suicide are the outcomes of the efforts of majority cultures to abolish traditional lifeways. These young people have faced new challenges that came with the elements and by human hand — floods, hailstorms, mold, petrochemical poisons.

Yet they live and, often, thrive.

As students, they participate in the life of school days and in the sports of cross country, gymnastics, hockey, lacrosse, soccer, skateboarding, skiing, snowshoeing, swimming and in choir, science classes, student council and Future Business Leaders of America. Many mention reading as a favorite activity.

As Indigenous students they also learn, participate in and long for their cultural traditions. They are Hoop dancers, Fancy dancers, Jingle dancers and drummers at powwows. They are artists who carve or use traditional materials to weave baskets or use Lego to create contemporary statements. They hunt, gather from the sea, study and speak their Indigenous languages and participate in moose and goose calling. They eat the raw meat of newly killed four-footed creatures, and octopus, crabs, sea urchins and mushrooms.

Their bodies are not perfect. They have autism, learning differences, and many are marked by the true disabilities of contemporary Native life — alcoholism and diabetes. At age fifteen they can already choose to leave a life of drugs to embrace a new future. They acknowledge the grief of loss of language and traditional education models. They long for the simple gifts of modern life — a place to study and read, a place to cook. They seek out their sanctuaries and places of honesty such as the Native friendship centers where they find guitar lessons and support groups. They help us see that even within the stress of contemporary life, there is a place for ceremony, whether it is time on the land or the ritual ceremonies of the Full Moon, the Dark Moon, or prayer.

They are junior elders and they relate their tribal histories and modern political issues extending from the Seminole Wars; the hanging of Dakota men during the US Civil War; the Wounded Knee of 1890; the life and death of Métis leader Louis Riel; boarding/residential schools; Wounded Knee II and the American Indian Movement (AIM) of the

1970s up to the Truth and Reconciliation Commission and the Northern Gateway oil pipeline.

They give us advice:

- "It's your life. Find people who will help you live it."
- "If we don't take care of the earth there will be nothing left but mocking silence for what we could have saved."
- "My advice to other Native kids is to keep on going to cultural things. Even if you don't see the point right away. The culture will keep you clean and safe. It will give you something to do that's important, with people who really want you to do well..."
- "If the white world thinks Native kids are worthless, then the best answer we can give them is to become the best — the best athletes, the best scholars, the best lawyers, the best parents — whatever. Not for them. For ourselves. To protect ourselves from all those negative messages."
- "Anger is useful only if you use it to get yourself to do something positive."

They understand Indigenous lifestyles:

- "We don't have a problem with secrets. People here look after each other. There's always an open door. If you really don't want to be at home, someone will take you in."
- "Native youth are hungry to be connected to something. They can find that connection here, and in the traditions of their own communities. Sometimes they have to go looking for it, but as long as they believe it's out there, they'll find it."

And they are hopeful for their futures and the futures of

their peoples. They are social activists already, launching and sustaining anti-smoking campaigns, volunteering at the humane society, or speaking and singing at rallies protesting pipelines or at the United Nations Conference on Sustainable Development. They participate in competitions and organizations that are today's equivalent of tribal societies, such as a local American Idol competition, art festivals, Special Olympics, national science fairs, the UNITY conference and the air cadets. They create, and already are writing and acting, recording music, appearing in movies and performing at the Winter Olympics. They already are the leaders — the eleven-year-old who speaks at international gatherings, the UNITY conference leader, and the Cherokee National Youth Choir member.

And they are teaching us to dream — dreams tempered with reality and with the need to connect and serve: "If I had all the power in the universe, I'd take away the chemical plants, make the reserve a bit bigger and have everything clean and good again."

They see a place for themselves through possible careers in the military; as police officers; counselors for the addicted, victims of sexual assault or those with mental illnesses; as daycare workers, high-school math teachers, scientists, business owners, pilots, bakers, horse trainers or big-cat specialists.

Some have an optimism that doesn't deny the dark side of life: "There are big problems, but small bits of light can help." Some of the lives are less optimistic, as we hear from Native youth in a drug treatment center and a youth prison. However, there are those who are turning their lives around through initiatives such as the Southwest Conservation Corps' Ancestral Lands Office and the Bringing Back the Horses project.

To some, the future is wide open. The message may not be, to all, that it gets better, but that staying strong in one's Indigenous past and present is the best of all worlds: "We're going to keep moving forward. It's on us now."

And to all, the message extends beyond their own lives and experiences: "What we do, we do for the Native youth who will follow us, seven generations from now."

Loriene Roy

Author's Note

In the United States, 3.08 million people identify themselves as Indigenous. There are 565 federally recognized tribes. In Canada, there are 617 First Nations communities representing more than fifty nations. Life expectancy for Indigenous people in North America is still ten years less than that of their non-Indigenous counterparts. Indigenous people are more likely to live in poverty, more likely to get tuberculosis, more likely to die as infants and less likely to go to university.

But statistics don't tell us everything.

They don't tell us about the healing that is being done, about the books that are being written, the music being recorded, the languages being revived and the families who are rediscovering each other.

Statistics don't tell us about the kids who are learning from the struggle and courage of the people who went before them, about the countless hours spent in community organizing, and about the determination to create a better future that will honor the pain of the past.

This book includes a small sample of these kids.

Most of the interviews were conducted in person. A few were done over the phone. Generous families and community leaders all over North America allowed me into their homes, their schools, community centers and churches. It was a privilege to meet them and to be able to record the words of their children.

This book is not intended to be a comprehensive look at the situations faced by Indigenous youth today. Large sections of the community, such as the First Nations of Quebec, the California Mission Indians and the Indigenous peoples of Alaska and Hawaii, are not represented — not because of a lack of importance but because of the limitations of a single book.

During my writing career I have been able to meet with kids around the world whose lives have been turned upside down by people with money, power and education who ought to know better. Always, I have been enlightened by what these young people have to say. My heritage is English, Scottish and Irish, which means that there are things I simply cannot understand. The children in this book have a strong grasp of history, a clear understanding of the world around them and a hopeful vision of what the future could be.

I hope that everyone who reads this book will come away with a better understanding of the tremendous wealth of talent these eloquent young people can bring to the world.

Deborah Ellis

Introduction

In 1824, the US Department of War had a problem with Indians, so it created the Office of Indian Affairs, the forerunner to the Bureau of Indian Affairs (BIA). Over the following decades, Indigenous peoples were killed by design or by disease, were forced to leave their homeland under the 1830 Indian Removal Act, and their sources of food were slaughtered.

Yet, they didn't all die.

By the end of the Civil War, the thought was to get rid of the remaining Native Americans by making them become like white people. The federal government gave money to church organizations to create boarding schools.

One of the earliest was the Carlisle Indian Industrial School in Pennsylvania. It was founded by Richard Henry Pratt, who said, "A great general has said that the only good Indian is a dead one. I agree with the sentiment, but only in this: that all the Indian there is in the race should be dead. Kill the Indian in him and save the man."

The boarding schools were run in a military style. The students slept in barracks, spent hours drilling and marching and had every moment of their day controlled by bells. They were punished for speaking their own languages and for trying to run away. Punishments included whippings, being denied food and being locked in sheds. Hair was cut short or shaved off. Any signs of cultural heritage were taken away.

More and more schools were built. There were 4,651 students in Native boarding schools in 1880, and by 1900 there were 21,568. More than half of all school-aged Native kids were sent away to these institutions. Parents who refused to send their children would be punished by the Bureau of Indian Affairs, which would refuse them food and other necessities. The terrible living conditions in many communities, ravaged by smallpox, hunger and inadequate housing, pushed many parents to hope that their children might be better off in boarding schools. At least they would eat.

Called industrial schools, the emphasis was on discipline and work more than on education. Boys were taught trades like carpentry and farming. Girls were taught to sew. For many children, the loss of family, identity and the trauma of abuse canceled out any benefit of learning a new skill. Most left the schools ill equipped to earn a living in white society and robbed of the traditional knowledge that would allow them to feel at home in their own communities.

In Canada, the situation evolved in much the same way. Between the 1870s and 1996, about 150,000 First Nations, Métis and Inuit kids were sent to residential schools. In some cases, after the children were taken, their homes and villages were destroyed, so the children had no place to return to.

While some children had a positive experience at these schools — they were cared for by good people and received a good education — others had to deal with abuse from the people they should have been able to trust. Church officials would knowingly send abusive priests and teachers to remote residential schools where they could abuse kids with impunity. Some of the female students at residential schools became pregnant after being raped by teachers. The Mohawk Institute near Brantford, Ontario, was nicknamed the Mush

Hole by students because they were fed a watery porridge and other bad food.

Often families were not allowed to visit the schools, and students were not allowed to go home. Children died when they tried to escape. They died from illness, neglect and malnutrition. And they died from harsh physical punishment. Many of those deaths were not properly documented and their graves were not properly marked. Families never knew what happened to their children.

The impact of these schools was severe and wide-reaching. For a long time the shame of the abuse and loss of culture was not talked about, but showed itself in addictions, high suicide rates and domestic violence. Children who had grown up in these schools had no memories of their parents, so they did not know how to be parents themselves. Families continued to suffer.

As time went on, government policy shifted. Residential schools were closed, but that didn't mean minds were opened. The prevailing view was that if you were a Native parent, you were a bad parent, and your children would be better off being raised by whites.

Social workers who had no knowledge of First Nations culture would go into communities and take children, putting them in foster care without any due process, investigation or paperwork. Children who could run fast into the bush might escape. Their slower, younger brothers and sisters were often taken away and never seen again.

This program, known as the Sixties Scoop, saw more than 11,000 status Indians in Canada removed from their families between 1960 and 1990, and those are just the documented cases.

Among those who were actually adopted and did not remain in foster care or orphanages, 70 percent were adopted by non-Native parents. Seventy percent of those adoptions broke down, the children then drifting from foster home to foster home.

The Indian Adoption Project ran a similar program in the United States. For example, thousands of Navajo children were given to the Church of Jesus Christ of Latter-day Saints to become workers on their farms. Many others went into Catholic-run orphanages to await adoption. More children in care meant more money for the organizations taking care of them.

In both countries, children often had no chance to say goodbye to their parents. Their parents had no way to appeal, and no way to get their children back. While some children were adopted by good people who raised them in safe and loving homes, others were abused in their foster homes and orphanages. Many lost their sense of who they were and where they came from.

Attacking Indigenous languages was another way to make Native people disappear. Before European contact, it is estimated that there were more than three hundred Native languages spoken in North America. Today, only 150 of those languages can still be heard. Only twenty of those are spoken by children, which means that 130 languages are in grave danger of disappearing, soon and forever.

Inadequate diet, brought on by poverty and bad government policies, has led to skyrocketing rates of diabetes in First Nations communities. For thousands of years Indigenous people ate healthy food from the land such as fish, game, corn, beans and berries. Generations of farmers and hunters knew how to cultivate crops and provide meat in ways that the wildlife would be sustained. The rituals around the hunt and the harvest were part of the rich spiritual culture and cycle of life, providing clothes, tools and rites of passage.

When Europeans arrived, things started to change. The US government had a policy of slaughtering the great herds of buffalo to make way for the railroad and to speed up the extermination of the Indigenous people. When the nations were rounded up and forced onto reservations, often far from their traditional territories, the government promised to provide food in exchange for their land. That practice continues today in the form of commodity foods — generally canned and processed, and not an adequate replacement for fresh proteins and vegetables.

And if all that were not enough, Indigenous people were made to further disappear by becoming a source of amusement and entertainment for colonial powers. Explorers such as Columbus took Native people back to Europe to be displayed as objects of curiosity. Many died on these trips. Indigenous people were displayed at fairs in different parts of the world between 1880 and 1930. Organizers made them wear crude costumes and screech instead of speak to match the audience's expectations of savagery.

At the World's Fair in St. Louis in 1904, the BIA set up a pretend boarding school, complete with Native students. Fair-goers would peer in at the children sitting at desks and taking lessons. The Olympics were also held in St. Louis that year. Alongside the Olympic Games were the "Anthropology Games." Some of the Indigenous people who were on display at the fair were put into games they had never played, with rules explained in a language they didn't understand, against white players who were competing at the Olympic level, to try to show that the white race was superior.

Indigenous people protested these displays. Their leaders

wrote letters, pamphlets and articles and gathered petitions calling for a more accurate portrayal of their cultures.

In 1898 the Hiawatha Asylum for Insane Indians was created in Canton, South Dakota, by a decree from Congress. It closed in 1934 after imprisoning hundreds of people from many tribes, including children. There was no actual treatment. People lived in filth, with improper and insufficient food. They were beaten, shackled and abused by untrained staff who couldn't speak their language. A special section of the asylum was set up for tourists to come and watch what the inmates were up to. At least 121 people died in the asylum. Their cemetery has been turned into a golf course.

The children in this book have inherited this history. That they are here at all is a miracle. That they are strong, smart, brave and looking forward to a new future is a tribute to them and to the amazing communities they come from.

I do not think the measure of a civilization is how tall its buildings of concrete are, but rather how well its people have learned to relate to their environment and their fellow humans.

— Sun Bear, Chippewa Tribe

Tingo, 14

Many First Nations, Native American, Inuit and Métis people in Canada and the United States live in communities outside their home reservations. Some families have lived in cities for generations. Others leave their reserves to look for work, go to school, join their families or search for something else.

There are more than one hundred Native friendship centers in cities and smaller communities all across Canada. They provide recreation, language classes and a place to be with others who share common experiences, and where feasts, powwows and celebrations take place. In the United States, many cities have similar centers under different names. Events are often open to the public, and people are welcome to call or drop by to learn about the events they can be a part of.

I met Tingo at a center in Kelowna, British Columbia. Kelowna is a small city in the fertile Okanagan Valley. There are breathtaking views of the Rocky Mountains and walking paths along the lake that legend says is home to a monster called Ogopogo.

I was born in Kelowna. My mother was born in Cardston, Alberta. She's from the Blackfoot people. They are made up of three groups — the Siksika, the Blood and the Piegan. A lot of them were killed off by smallpox when the white settlers came. Others died when the whites killed off all the buffalo.

My father was born in Jinotega, Nicaragua. When he was fourteen he was involved in the civil war there. It was dangerous and he left. He made his way to the United States and lived there for a while. He had to come to Canada when things got harder for refugees in the US. He came here fifteen years ago, which is where he met my mother.

He loves to tell us stories of when he was a kid, running around in the jungle. A chicken saved his life once. There's a type of lizard in the jungle. If it touches you, it hurts and could kill you because of the poison in its skin. One of these little lizards dropped down out of the tree and landed on my dad's shirt. He could feel the poison starting to burn his skin, but he was afraid to brush it off because then he'd have to touch it. Then, suddenly, a chicken flew up and ate the lizard. So a chicken saved his life.

My parents don't live together now. My father puts stucco on houses when he can find the work, or does any other job people will hire him for. My mother doesn't have a job.

Things got bad at home last year. My father couldn't find work and we were always short of money. There was a lot of fighting in the house. It got so bad that my brother and I went to stay with our grandmother for three days.

On the third day my father picked us up and we went to the office of a social service agency for a meeting with a lady. This lady said we could choose. Do we want to live with our mother or with our father? Well, my father was sitting right there and I didn't want to hurt his feelings so I said I want to live with Dad. My little brother wanted to stay with me.

We stayed with Dad for a month. He had no money for an apartment so the three of us stayed in a motel room, the cheapest one we could find. It smelled funny. The motel was close to school, close enough to walk, but that's the only good thing I can say about it.

It's very hard to live in a motel. You can't run around anywhere. You have to be quiet or the other people will complain to the management and you'll get thrown out.

Food is hard, too. We just ate canned food, sandwiches, nothing like real meals. You never really feel like you've eaten when you eat that stuff. And your body doesn't feel right. Although I remember once we got one of those barbecue chickens at the grocery store, already cooked. We had to eat the whole thing because we didn't have a fridge to keep the leftovers in, but it tasted really good.

My brother has FASD [fetal alcohol spectrum disorder]. Before he was born, he got brain damage from my mother's drinking. He's very smart. He's really good at math and spelling, all the school subjects, really. He looks like a regular kid. But it's hard for him to sit still and listen so he gets frustrated and he gets into trouble all the time. Teachers don't really see him. They just see a problem. I try to watch out for him.

It was really hard for him in the motel because he likes to cook. It calms him down and he's good at it. He likes to make chili, spaghetti and bannock.

We couldn't do our homework very well in the motel. There was no place to do it because we had all our stuff with us, so it was either the bed or the floor, and the floor was gross. The teachers weren't that understanding about it. They just said Do it at school then, after class. That was really hard because I had to keep an eye on my brother, and after sitting in school all day he was not able to sit another minute to do homework! The one thing I was doing at that time that I liked was doing drawings for the school newspaper. It helped me feel normal.

After a month of this, Dad couldn't find work and he ran out of money. He couldn't pay the money for the motel room and he couldn't even feed us. So we went into foster care. We were there for something like nine months.

I was pretty nervous. I didn't know the people. I didn't know what they expected and what would annoy them. I didn't want to get in the way so I didn't ask them for much, like extra food if I wanted more at dinner. It took a while, but eventually I relaxed. The foster parents were really nice. They knew I liked chocolate, and so they'd always keep these big jugs of chocolate milk in the fridge, and they didn't care how much I drank.

My brother doesn't talk to people he doesn't know, so he mostly stayed quiet. They gave him lots of space and didn't nag him, which is what he needed.

Now we stay with Mom during the week and with Dad on the weekends.

When I'm not in school I spend a lot of time here at this friendship center. They serve good meals here, for free. We came here to eat as often as we could when we lived in the motel. It got us through.

On Mondays I come here for guitar lessons. On Wednesdays we do Sister Talk and Brother Talk, which are groups where we discuss what's on our mind and learn about our culture. On Thursdays I'm a leader of the Turtle Huddle group. This is for younger kids. We do crafts with them, like make drums and rattles, traditional things. And we play games. On Fridays we have youth group. Just social. With food, of course!

At Sister Talk and Brother Talk, we do a family systems program, looking at what a family should be like, how people should treat each other. We learned how to do a genogram, which is like a family history. We do it to look for the troubles in our families — the troubles that have become secrets.

We talk a lot about grief because that's been a big part of our lives as Native people — grief over losing our land, our language, our customs, our ways. Grief often comes out as trouble.

My father's childhood was all war, and he's told me about that. And my mother's life has been hard. And my mother's parents — their life was even harder with what they went through, and there weren't places like this to help them. I've never met my Nicaraguan grandparents, but I know their life was hard too, living under a dictator who liked to torture people. Sometimes I felt like I was carrying all that sorrow with me. Learning about grief is hard. You have to be honest with yourself, and that's not easy. Grief is something you'd rather not think about. You'd rather pretend it wasn't there. And there's no real cure for it, except to speak it and share it and honor what you've lost.

When I was younger, I used to keep family secrets, secrets about things that had happened, things that had gone wrong. In the group we all wrote our secrets down on pieces of paper and burned them. We stood in a circle and prayed while we watched them burn. All the secrets went up to the Creator. I watched them go up in smoke and felt a great release. It was like, now the Creator knows our secrets and will carry them for us.

School is better this year. The teachers have given me extra help and now I'm all caught up.

I like being a leader in the Turtle Huddle group. Sometimes I look back on the good times I used to have as a little kid and it makes me want to be little again, but it's good to have responsibilities too.

I'm taking drawing lessons from Dennis Weber, an amazing Native artist who teaches at the Métis center. I'm learning the basic shapes. In the last class we learned about the shapes of skulls, like a buffalo skull is in the shape of a triangle.

I go to ceremonial events too, like the Sun Dance. And I go to sweat lodges. The sweat lodge is a place for praying. It's a very old and sacred thing to do.

I've learned from all this that it's going to be okay. Try not to worry too much. Try to do your best to look for things that are bigger than you. And if you meet people who treat you badly, don't give them too much power. They might change and they might not, but you don't have to hang around them and wait to see how it's going to turn out.

It's your life. Find people who will help you live it.

Mari, 14

Tobacco is a native crop, first used by Indigenous people for ceremonial purposes. After the arrival of the Europeans, it was grown as a cash crop. The money the settlers got for their crop helped fund the American Revolution. Even George Washington grew tobacco. It grew more popular, and the invention of the cigarette-making machine meant that hundreds of thousands — then millions — of cigarettes could be produced every day, even after everyone realized how bad smoking was for people's health. A new product needed a new market.

In Canada, under Section 87 of the Indian Act, Aboriginal people do not have to pay tax on personal property. Canadian cigarettes for non-Aboriginals are heavily taxed — called a "sin tax" to discourage smoking and to help cover the extra health-care costs incurred by smokers (health care being paid for by the government in Canada). The government decides how many tax-free cigarettes each reserve will use and ships them to on-reserve dealers. Although the cheap cigarettes are supposed to be sold only to reserve residents, some see it as a way to make money by selling to anyone. Tax-free smoke shops have become a regular feature on many reserves.

Many Indigenous communities in Canada and the United States are working to encourage the traditional use of tobacco, producing products that are all-natural and chemical free for use in religious ceremonies.

Mari comes from Minneapolis, Minnesota. One-third of Minnesota's Native Americans live in the Twin Cities of St. Paul/Minneapolis, and 15 percent more live in the suburbs of those cities.

I was born in Minneapolis, and I'm part of the Leach Lake Ojibwe. I go to a classical private school. We study humane letters, logic, Latin, writing, algebra, the Bible, theology, the classics like *The Odyssey* and *The Confessions of St. Augustine*. I like humane letters the best.

I feel more Ojibwe than American because I do all the traditions and follow the culture. I do the Full Moon ceremony to celebrate a woman's moon time and I do the Dark Moon ceremony, which is like a sweat but in a dark room.

It makes me feel happy to do these things. Whether it's me doing it today or another Ojibwe woman doing it five hundred years ago, it ties me in with her and with all the other Ojibwe. It makes me feel hopeful, like the traditions will continue.

My mother works with the Division of Indian Work. It's a non-profit organization that works with American Indians in Minneapolis around health and social problems. She does things like teen pregnancy prevention, helping women give birth in the traditional way, youth leadership, housing, all kinds of things.

I've been working on this anti-smoking project with some other Native kids. The program is called Mashkiki Ogichidaag, which means Medicine Warriors.

Tobacco is part of our culture. We use it for spiritual things, like when we burn it with prayers, our prayers are carried upwards to the Creator. It wasn't something to use all day, every day. When we're out on the land, we leave tobacco behind as a thank-you to the earth. It's a special thing to give tobacco as a gift. It's a sign of respect. Traditional Native tobacco is all natural. The stuff in cigarettes is all poison and chemicals.

My people use tobacco now in ways that are not traditional and are not good for us. It causes cancer and breathing problems like emphysema. It also makes a mess.

A lot of smokers are not very careful about what they do with their cigarette butts. They just throw them anywhere. I don't know if they don't think the butts are garbage, or if they also throw garbage everywhere, but I've noticed a lot of smokers are just messy about this.

I got tired of seeing cigarette butts tossed around. They look ugly and they're not natural and so all they do is hurt the environment. They're poison! Dogs could eat them, birds could get bits of that poison tobacco when they're hunting around for insects or worms. Little kids too little to know any better could be crawling around the park, pick up a cigarette butt and put it in their mouths, because little kids put everything into their mouths! It could make them very sick, with upset stomachs or seizures or even worse. You'd think smokers would think about stuff like that before they toss their butt away on the ground. How much energy would it take for them to just throw their cigarette butt into a garbage can? Some adults are lazy.

My mother believes we are responsible for the earth and for each other, and that when there's a problem, we all need to pitch in to fix it.

A few of us kids got together and made a plan. We started out by making a presentation to Mom's colleagues about people not smoking on the grounds of their office, so that it's a clean, healthy place for people to come to.

Then we went into a public park to pick up cigarette butts. We took empty tin cans with us, and spent a very sunny afternoon going around the park and collecting up all the butts smokers had just tossed into the grass. We took all the cigarette butts to a meeting of the parks board and showed them how many there were, and we explained what the dangers are.

I think they were surprised. I think they already knew about the dangers of cigarettes — at least, I hope so! — but I think they were surprised that we felt so strongly about it.

The parks board meetings are shown on local cable TV, so I knew a lot of people would be watching when I and another kid from the group stepped up to the podium. As the project leader, I did the speaking, and I showed all the butts we had picked up. There were other groups there too that night, all asking for the same thing.

And we won! The new policy is that no one can smoke now in public parks in Minneapolis!

I've done other presentations too — to schools, to youth groups, to the All Nations Indian Church. I went to a media training day to learn how to create public service announcements. I keep learning new things so that I can keep doing new things. Other kids come and go from the group — their lives get busy with other things — but there are always new ways to recruit new kids to keep the project going.

This is an easy thing for kids everywhere to do. If adults are smoking in a park or outside a hospital or a church or whatever, you can go and pick up the butts and get the newspaper to come and take pictures, and maybe the adults will be so ashamed they'll throw their cigarette butts in the garbage where they belong.

I guess I have a different kind of idea of what's fun. Picking up other people's garbage is not fun, but making things better is.

When I'm not doing this kind of work and I'm not in school, I play soccer. I have asthma, but I don't care about that. I just play.

I like to sing too. We had an American Idol-type competition, called Franklin Avenue Idol, and I entered. I sang an Etta James song and people really liked it. I also performed at the Native American Arts Festival. Plus I love to design clothes. So I do lots of things.

The more I do, the more I want to do.

A lot of Native Americans are stressed out. Not a lot have steady jobs. The economy is bad for many people, and it's really bad for Native Americans. I want people to be kind to each other and treat each other well. That would make it easier for everyone.

Mashkiki Ogichidaag youth have produced four anti-smoking videos: "Second-hand Smoke at Work," "Cigarette Butts Clean Up," "What Would You Rather Be Doing?" and "What Our Community Has to Say." They can be seen on YouTube.

Jason, 15

Nipissing First Nation Reserve is on the north shore of Lake Nipissing in Ontario. Roughly 2,500 people are registered as belonging to the community, and 900 of them live on the reserve in several small villages. They are of the Anishinabek Nation, descendants of the ancient Nipissing, Ojibwe and Algonquin peoples. In 1615 they were "discovered" by Samuel de Champlain, although archeologists have evidence they were in the area for at least 9,400 years before the Europeans arrived. They ate pickerel and whitefish from the lake and hunted in the forest.

Nbisiing Secondary School is teaching the new generation of Anishinabek leaders. Academic studies are combined with traditional teachings and ceremonies.

Jason is a student at this school.

I was born in Toronto. My father is from Nipissing First Nation near North Bay, Ontario. I don't know where my mother is from.

I lived with my mom until I was two. Then I moved to the reserve and lived with my grandmother. Then my grandmother died and I went to live with an aunt.

My mom took off. I don't know where she is and I don't want to know.

I'm good at science but not at math. I hold a lot of scientific theories in my head. I can see them there clearly, like drawings. Science is beautiful. All science — space science, biology, chemistry. All of it.

I used to go to a Catholic school in town that was mixed Native and white kids. I was in a mainstream class until grade four. Then they put me in special ed. I understand the concepts behind the work, but I have trouble letting people know I understand. They need proof. They can't just take my word for it. I've been back and forth to Sick Kids hospital in Toronto for testing. They're looking into learning disabilities. So far they've come up with a label of autism PDD [Pervasive Development Disorder].

I didn't care about going to special ed. I mean, I didn't feel bad about it. It was more comfortable than being around kids who thought they were perfect.

And sometimes I'd hear teachers say things like Stupid Indian kids, or Those Indian kids give us so many problems. Not all the teachers. But it just takes one to give you a really bad day.

Now I'm in the high school on Nipissing Reserve. It's a mainstream high school, not special ed, but the teachers take the time to help us learn. They work with us to find out how we learn best. It's a small school too. No one gets lost in the crowd. We call our teachers by their first names. We can eat in class if we get hungry. We can feel that the teachers respect us and really want us to do well, so it's easy to have a positive attitude. There's a sign on the door of the teachers' room that says: They may not remember everything that we teach them, but they will always remember how we treat them.

And that's true. We all have stories from being in mixed schools. White teachers calling us Wagon Burners or doing some stupid fake-Indian craft like making war bonnets. Hearing kids say racist things to us and not doing anything to stop it, like it's no big deal. Or teachers that expect us to be stupid because we're Native, so if we're struggling with math or something they don't make a lot of effort to show us we can do it.

I wasn't around my father or mother much when I was growing up, but I know the bad choices they made. It feels like I'm on the outside of their lives looking in, and I can see how the mistakes they made have affected their lives and their family's lives. I look at them for who they are and what they've done and I don't like it.

Mom's gone, somewhere. Dad's gone too. I know where he is but I don't have much to do with him. It would have been nice to have had them both around looking after me and watching me grow up, but what's the point of wishing that?

I'm doing okay. I live in a more isolated part of the reserve, only three houses. Me and my aunt are in one, my uncle is in another. He has his own wood mill set up there. The area is called Mosquito Creek.

It's great. I can ride my ATV and not bother anybody. I have a pet husky named Copper. He was a golden color when I first got him. Now he's gray. He stays outside. He's used to rough living.

Since my dad's mother and my mom's mother both died, I have no grandmother in my life. That leaves a real empty place, to be without a grandmother. But a few of the grandmothers of the Ojibwe tradition have adopted me as their grandson. Every kid needs grandparents, either blood ones or adopted ones.

People contribute themselves to me, so I try to pass that

along and contribute to others. In North Bay I'm involved with Special Olympics, helping out with lots of activities. When I volunteer, people treat me with respect. In Sturgeon Falls, when I was younger, I experienced a lot of racism. Adults, mostly, giving me racism on the street or when I went into a store. Grown people who are really ignorant, more ignorant than kids but they get to vote and run the country. Go figure. People gave me their bad attitudes. I tried to tune it out and pretend it wasn't there. I know I should always stand up and say something, but racists won't see it that way and they're likely to come after me. And a lot of the people who believe the stereotypes about Aboriginal people don't think they're being racist, and they get really mad if you point their ignorance out to them.

But I hate it when I'm walking down the sidewalk, minding my own business, and some white adult calls me filthy racist names. It interrupts my day. It happened more when I was smaller. Now that I'm bigger, the white cowards don't risk it.

I used to have anger problems when I was younger, probably because I was having trouble learning. I'm lucky to not be on any meds. I know lots of kids who are on meds to control their behavior. I'm learning how to manage my own temper and I have the self-discipline to get me where I want to be.

Xavier, 10

Formal education has histori-
cally been a way to oppress
Indigenous people in North
America. Forcing children into
residential schools, separating them from their traditional
languages, culture, foods and
customs, separating them
from their land and families
was bad enough. In addition, the physical and sexual
abuse that happened in many schools, where there
were often harsh living conditions, poor diets and ex-
posure to diseases, has led many generations to have
a negative view of formal education. This in turn has
led to high drop-out rates for Indigenous students
across North America.

Through the efforts of many people, this has started to change. There are universities for Indigenous
students, such as the First Nations University in Saskatchewan and Haskell Indian Nations University in
Kansas. Aboriginal centers in universities provide a
gathering place for students, a place to feel at home
away from home. Laurentian University piloted a program that allowed First Nations students to earn university credits while they were still in high school, to
give them the confidence to go on and complete a
degree. Some elementary schools have made a com-
mitment to showcase and celebrate all the cultures
represented by the student body, including Indige-

neous cultures. And there are mentorship programs, scholarships and a growing job market for young professionals.

Xavier is a young man just at the beginning of his journey.

I'm a member of the Nez Perce tribe of Idaho, although we moved to Spokane, Washington, when I was just a baby. I was born in Lewiston, which is right next to the reservation. I love going back there to visit my grandparents. I also love living in the city.

I'm proud to be from the Nez Perce tribe because it is the tribe of Chief Joseph, one of the great chiefs. They found gold on our land a long time ago and the government took our land away. They told the Nez Perce to leave but of course they didn't want to. The army came and Chief Joseph was afraid everyone would be killed. So he led his people on a long march. Even then the soldiers kept coming. They kept wanting to kill the Native people so that the white people could get the gold.

Really, I'm a mixture of people. My father's father is African American. I'm also part Mexican. My great-grandfather was José Hernandez. He died before I was born.

I'm in fifth grade. Math is okay, but I sometimes have trouble with fractions. I like reading best, especially books by Andrew Clements. He wrote *Frindle*.

My father's name is Raphael. He's a university professor. My mother's name is Gloria. She has a master's of social work. I have two older sisters and two younger sisters, and I'm right in the middle.

It's because of my sister Sophie that I got into running. She was doing cross country, but my dad didn't want her walking home from practice by herself. So I started tagging along with her so she wouldn't be alone. Then I decided to start running just to pass the time while I waited for her. And I discovered I liked it.

I didn't win my first race, but I came in second. Then I got second in an all-city mile run.

Sophie doesn't do cross country anymore. She does dance — ballet — which is also hard work.

I train with the Spokane Mercury Track Club. My events are the 200, the 400 and the 800 yard runs. We're divided into age groups. Spokane has lots of good parks for running. I run these races and I practice and I run on the treadmill too. Plus I play basketball and football. I really love football.

My family are all athletes. My father played basketball at Lapwai High School on the reservation, and then he played for Eastern Washington University. That's where he teaches now. My mom played sports all through high school. She went to the same school as my dad. That's how they met. She got an all-state award in basketball. She also played baseball and volleyball. Lapwai is a town on the reservation. It means Land of the Butterflies.

My mom's dad was Larry McFarlane Sr. He died in 1971. He was a really good man and served in the military. My Gramma Rosa is still alive. She played sports in school too. I have a step-grandfather, Papa John.

My grampa on my father's side, Jeff Guillory, played football with the Dallas Cowboys.

All these people in my family doing things makes me want to try harder and do more, so that they'd be proud of me. And because my parents are big on education, I want to do well in school too.

I love going back to the reservation on holidays to see my

Gramma Rosa and my Gramma Connie and my grandfathers and all my cousins. Lots of cousins. We have a whole lot of fun. We can see big hills behind Gramma Rosa's house. There's woods to play in. We make forts, play in the creek, run around in all the space. It's not like the city. There's room and silence and not a lot of cars. You feel really free there.

It doesn't make a difference to people in Spokane that I'm Native. In sports it's all about the sport, not about who's white and who's Native or whatever. But there is something special about being on the reservation and you're surrounded by people who have your blood and the same history.

There are white people on the reservation too. They farm some of the land and pay rent to the tribe. I don't know if there are any problems. I don't pay attention to that anyway. When I'm there I'm too busy playing with my cousins.

I'm starting to learn how to run. In the beginning, when I first started doing long runs, I'd go into a sprint right from the start, and then I'd get too tired to keep it up. But now I start slow and keep that pace, then I have lots of energy left to do a fast sprint at the very last. The other runners don't see me coming!

It's very exciting to go to the big races, with everybody in the stands cheering for all the runners. I get a nervous feeling in my stomach. I don't eat too much before the race. Just a snack and I drink water. When I'm not racing, my favorite food is spaghetti.

I've won some races. First place, second place. Last summer I went to the USATF National Junior Olympic Track and Field Championships in Wichita, Kansas. I brought home a medal. It was really intense. For a competition like that, you can't eat junk food or stay up late if you want to do a good run. You should eat a lot of protein and get enough rest.

It was intense but it was also fun. I liked hanging out with the other athletes, these other kids who liked to run and do things. It was cool being with that many runners from all over. Before the 400 meet, there was a storm, and it got rained out for a while. We all hung out. It was a really good time.

My parents make sure we know all about our history and our culture — all of our cultures. We're a pretty busy family, and we don't waste a lot of time on things that aren't important. Although I do like playing this really old video game of Dad's. It's called Technoball and it's from a really long time ago, like 1991.

As I get older I want to continue to be an athlete and continue to get good grades. Of course I'm going to go to college. I want to end up with some sort of big-time job. Engineering, business, some kind of big career like that. And I'll keep playing sports.

Children were encouraged to develop strict discipline and a high regard for sharing. When a girl picked her first berries and dug her first roots, they were given away to an elder so she would share her future success. When a child carried water for the home, an elder would give compliments, pretending to taste meat in water carried by a boy or berries in that of a girl. The child was encouraged not to be lazy and to grow straight like a sapling.

— Mourning Dove (Christine Quintasket), Salish

Pearl, 15

Kashechewan First Nation is a Cree reserve near James Bay in northern Ontario. During the summer, the only way in or out is by plane or barge or freighter canoe. There are winter roads when the temperatures are low enough for packed-down ice and snow. In recent years, climate change has led to warmer winters. The ice roads don't stay frozen as long as they used to, and badly needed goods like kerosene are not able to get into the community.

Seventeen hundred people live in Kashechewan — descendants of people who roamed the land hunting and fishing. The community has had to deal with high rates of youth suicide. In January 2007, twenty-one young people tried to kill themselves, one as young as nine years old. In late 2012, the chief declared a state of emergency. With winter closing in, the community was running out of fuel, and twenty-one homes were not fit to live in during the cold weather.

Pearl lives in Kashechewan.

Kashechewan is a small reserve. The roads are rough and narrow. We have a few houses that have been renovated and are in okay shape but most are not. The Band has been working at getting the homes better for the last three years.

Some kids think there's nothing to do on the reserve and

that's why they get into drugs. I started smoking grass when I was eleven. I saw my older sister do it. Then I tried it and got addicted to it. I smoked it for a lot of years.

It wasn't hard to stop once I made the decision to. I told myself it wasn't good for me and I don't want to die at an early age.

Marijuana is around. People go out to the south and bring it in. I think people do drugs because they have losses in their family or losses in their spirit and they need to forget their pain for a while.

Or they can't find anything else to do. That's not my problem. I think there's lots to do. I go for walks along the dyke that holds back James Bay. I go out in the bush, go for picnics.

The reserve used to flood all the time. When my father was little it was really bad. I also remember floods happening. The whole community would gather on the big hill on the baseball field to get out of the way of the rising water. Graveyards would get flooded. They still do. The water treatment center would break down.

Our drinking water is safe now. A few years ago we had E. coli in the water, which can kill you. They sent us all out of the reserve. We had to go. It was an evacuation. Still, people got sick. They got terrible rashes and bad stomachs and got very weak.

Then later I was evacuated out to Stratford with my family. That's in the southern part of Ontario. We didn't choose where we went. The Band office made all the arrangements and that's where they found that would accept us. We stayed in the arena. I slept in the curling rink on a mat on the floor. The town was really welcoming to us. A lady came and took some of us out to her farm for the day so we could enjoy her animals. A man from a nearby reserve came and showed us some First Nations medicines and gave us sweetgrass.

We didn't go to school while we were there. We just hung out. I went for walks around the town with my friends.

I remember seeing Justin Bieber but he wasn't so famous then. I was in an ice-cream shop trying to decide what to get. He was in the line behind me. I thought I was taking too long because I couldn't make up my mind. I told him to go ahead of me. He was really nice. He said, "Go ahead, take your time, no problem." I remembered him because he was so kind and then later I saw him on TV.

I'd never been that far south before. I was born in Thunder Bay and I'd been to Timmins when my sister was born. Mostly I've been on the reserve.

The south has a lot of rules and a lot of laws and a lot of noise.

I prefer up north. It gets nice and cold in the winter. I can go snowshoeing and skidooing.

We go winter camping too. We stay in tents. We have a woodstove in the tent that dies out at three in the morning. I have to get up and feed it so we don't freeze.

I go hunting geese with my father in the winter. We sit and wait and talk in quiet voices. We see the trees, the little birds chirping. We see little seals. I've caught three seals.

I know about guns. I use a 20-gauge shotgun, which is bigger than a 12-gauge. It's really big. I taught myself to shoot by first using a BB gun and aiming at cans.

With geese you shoot fast and aim at the head. I've been shooting geese since I was six.

I do most of the work. I learned when I was little how to pluck the goose, cut it open, take out the organs, cook it on the fire, chop the wood for the fire, go into the bush to find the wood — all of it. It's a natural thing for young women to do. In the south, kids are not allowed to do anything except watch TV.

I like being up north because I'm not lazy. I can be healthy. I'll be able to tell my kids and grandkids about my adventures and show them how they can do the same things.

Up north we eat food from the land and food that's shipped in. I don't eat a lot, just little amounts every day, enough to fuel me.

I love helping the elders, chopping wood, cleaning their yards. It's a sign of respect to do things for them. Whenever we go hunting we bring back geese for them. Or I can give them a ride, like a taxi, but without paying. I don't have a driver's license. No one on my reserve cares about that. I taught myself to drive. Some days I'll borrow a relative's truck and drive around looking for elders who need a ride.

I taught myself how to draw as well. I like to draw Native art, things from nature. I get drawing tips from school, then I keep working on it until I get it right.

I'm a writer as well. Whenever I'm bored and have nothing to do, I get a scrap of paper and write down what's on my mind. I show these thoughts to my mom, but mostly I keep them private. I write poetry too. I just write down what my heart is saying and it comes out like a poem.

I'm good at school. I was an honor student in grade six.

In grade seven I missed a lot of school because I was always out in the wild. I still go when I can. Sometimes to hunt, sometimes to just be there.

I go alone into the bush. I have this place I've been to a lot with my grandfather. When we go together we just sit and talk. When I go alone the animals come up to me. I sit very still so they're not afraid. They think I'm just part of the forest. I bring food for them. Squirrels, raccoons, fox. I feed them and talk to them.

This place is our land. There are beautiful trees around me. Me and Grampa built benches using just wood, without nails. He taught me to make fire without matches or lighters, using rocks to make sparks on grass and adding wood slowly. It's all about taking time and not rushing things when you're in the wild.

When I'm out in the bush by myself I have no worries. I know I can care for myself. I can find meat and cook it. Sometimes I don't even bother to cook it. I just eat it raw. If I don't hunt I'll take meat from home — bear, moose, caribou, deer, beaver. It's all healthier to eat raw.

My parents are both from the north and they had a good experience of school. But my grandparents went to residential school and it was not good. They got hit when they spoke their language. The nuns told them to wash their faces with Javex bleach because their skin was dark. My grandparents were taken far away from their families when they were four and didn't get back home again until they were eighteen. They couldn't go home to visit. They simply lost their parents and their parents lost them.

But my grandparents were smart. They didn't listen to the nuns. They kept speaking their language when the nuns and priests weren't around. They weren't brainwashed.

My grandfather is a windtalker. He prays and speaks to the wind and gets answers. He goes out with a hand drum when it is very windy and sings.

When I'm older I'm going to be a Sun dancer. That's a Cree person who dances for three days without eating or drinking. You dance this in the wild, when the sun is bright orange in the evening. I'm already a Fancy Shawl dancer and

I can sing with a hand drum in my first language.

I'm a youth counselor on my reserve. I work with kids ages ten to twelve. We do all kinds of activities, share stories, do things to keep them busy. They come to me for advice sometimes. I tell them that we may struggle, but all they need to do is to make the right choices.

I plan to stay in school, get a job, travel and see the world. You can meet different people that way, share your stories and make friends.

I'm thinking of going into police work. On my reserve, the police are lazy. If I become a police officer I'll never use a car. I'll walk around and know what's going on and people will know that they can trust me.

What is life? It is the flash of a firefly in the night. It is the breath of a buffalo in the winter time. It is as the little shadow that runs across the grass and loses itself in the sunset.

— Crowfoot, Blackfoot Confederacy

Myleka, 13, and Tulane, 14

The Navajo Nation is the largest Indigenous nation in the United States, both in land size and in population. It takes in parts of Arizona, Utah and New Mexico and has 250,000 citizens.

But Navajo history has been marked by painful and traumatic events. During the 1860s, the US Army waged war on the Navajo by destroying their live-stock and crops, driving the people to starvation. In 1864, large numbers of Navajo were forced marched hundreds of miles from their traditional territories to Bosque Redondo in New Mexico, in what is known as the Long Walk. Many died.

In 1930, a US Senate committee admitted that churches were kidnapping Navajo children and forc-ing them into boarding schools — the churches re-ceived more government money if they had more chil-dren. Then, in 1951, huge deposits of uranium were discovered under Navajo land. The government em-ployed Navajo miners but did not give them protec-tive gear and proper ventilation. The water the miners were given to drink was radioactive. When they got sick from radiation, they were fired. High rates of lung cancer among former miners and their families were due to these practices. The mine companies left huge piles of radioactive waste on the reservation, going bankrupt as soon as they were told to clean it up.

Yet the Navajo culture thrives today. Navajo arts are known worldwide. Blankets, pottery, rugs, jewelry and sand paintings are traditionally made using the natural materials found in the desert and mountains.

Tulane and Myleka live in Kayenta, Arizona, on the Navajo reservation. They are part of a new generation of artists.

Myleka

My brother and I were chosen to create artwork for the poster for the 90th annual Santa Fe Indian Market. Every August, a thousand or so Native artists gather to show and sell their work. It's amazing. Thousands and thousands of people come to it. They have never had young artists create the poster before. My brother and I were the first.

We had to submit our work to some judges. We submitted five pieces each, and the judges chose both of us! Tulane's piece is a mask made out of Legos. Mine had four circles in it, one on top of the other. They both have colors from the earth and sky, and they go really well together.

My design came to me in a vision when I did my Kinaaldá. This is a ceremony Navajo girls do to mark our coming of age, becoming women. It goes on for days. I went through it when I turned twelve. You get up very early, before the sun. You sing at night, grind corn, do prayers and ceremonies. It's a very sacred, special thing. It helps you grow into a strong woman. My mother went through it. My grandmother too, and probably her mother and grandmother way back through the generations. You do it so the gods can know you. You do it because you are Navajo.

At the end of my ceremony I was told I would receive

something from the Creator, and I received the vision of the circles. I felt really honored.

I come from a family of artists. My father, Alvin John, is a very famous artist, and he and my mother, Iverna Parrish-John, got us started. They didn't push us, but art supplies were always around when we were growing up. I think we are all born with the love of making art, but most people tell themselves that art is a childhood thing, not something to do when they get older. When really it's something people can love doing all their lives even if they have some other job they do that brings in money.

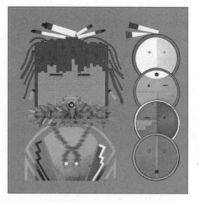

Artwork for the Santa Fe Indian Market poster.

My dad does amazing work. He paints, he sculpts with steel, he did this big mural near the Navajo transportation headquarters. He's really well respected. My uncle is also an artist. His name is Melvin L. John and my Uncle David has an art gallery in Santa Fe. We learn from all of them, but we also go our own way.

My mother works as a lab technician at the health clinic here on the reservation. We used to live in Phoenix, but we moved here not long ago because she got that job.

It was a big change moving here from Phoenix, and sometimes I miss the city, but overall living here is a good experience. It's different from what most kids get to experience, so I'm lucky. Plus, it's beautiful! It is SO beautiful! There's lots of natural light and not a lot of noise.

I'm attending Kayenta Middle School. I'm on the basketball team — the KMS Colts. The other students know about the art that I do, and they think it's interesting. Even the teachers ask me how I do things in art. In college I think I'll study design. I'd like to design clothes as part of my career. Or maybe be a nurse.

I'd love it if other people would keep doing art all through their lives, even if they don't think they're good at it. Art helps you to see things.

Tulane

I just started high school at Monument Valley High, and I like it. I play basketball, football and do track. I'm with my own people. It's a Navajo high school, so I'm with other Navajo kids. I've been to mixed schools, and I like this better. I guess it's better because we're with our own people. There's things we just understand. We don't have to be explaining all the time.

My father's parents didn't get to go to school. My grandfather was a railroad worker for thirty years. He did sandpainting as a spiritual practice and a cultural expression. My grandmother spoke only Navajo. She did traditional weaving and took care of the family. Because of that she was cut off from attending school. My great-grandfather was a blacksmith and a medicine man. He worked with his hands and was very traditional. My father says they were gifted both traditionally and spiritually. I wish I could have met them. Where my grandparents came from, there's still no running water and the community only just got electricity.

I like school. My parents also liked school. My mother's parents did not have a good experience of school. They were sent to a Christian boarding school where they were told they were only allowed to speak English. The only language they knew when they went in was Navajo, and they got beaten for speaking it. So you can imagine, it was not good.

My art inspiration comes from a lot of places. When I was a kid I loved cartoons and comics and playing with Legos. My folks took me to Legoland and I couldn't believe what I was seeing! All the possibilities! So now I use a lot of Legos in my paintings, and I bring them into traditional symbols.

For the Santa Fe art show poster I did a painting in acrylics and Legos. I did a Yébîchai head made of Legos on canvas. I've done several pieces like that. I found out that some people from the Lego corporation wanted to buy one of my pieces, but a Navajo family wanted it more, so they got it.

My sister is really talented. She uses all sorts of materials in her art too. She's made Navajo dolls out of felt and tinfoil. She does sand paintings of yé'iis. She's won all sorts of awards. We both have. The good thing about awards is that they open up more opportunities to learn and to create in new ways.

The Santa Fe festival was amazing. It is so big! All kinds of nations were there — Navajo, Cherokee, Shoshone, Penobscot, Ojibwe, Pueblo. So many! Baskets, dolls, paintings, jewelry, clothing, ceremonial pieces, modern sculpture. There were films, there was food. It was hard to take it all in. I had so much fun! I spent a lot of time in our booth watching people look at our art, talking with people. People wanted to take pictures of us and have us sign their posters. I know that art isn't about that kind of thing and that's not why I want to keep doing it, but I had a great time.

I love living on the reservation. We live right by Monument Valley. It's breathtaking. It's a famous place because a lot of Western movies were shot there. And we get to see it every day.

I'd like to study architecture at university — maybe at Stanford or the University of Kentucky. And of course I'll keep learning about art.

My parents stress how important it is for us to learn traditional values like respect for our elders. Native people used to be told they had to forget who they were and what they knew. Like my grandparents being told they had to forget their language. That time is over. We are remembering all that wisdom and learning from it and building on it.

There are a lot of ways to get distracted from who we really are. Art helps us find our way back.

Valene, 18

In the 1960s, it became common practice for the Canadian government to "scoop" Indigenous children from their homes and put them into the care of the state. This became known as the Sixties Scoop.

Although the official government policies that led to the Sixties Scoop are over, it's hard to tell. The number of Indigenous children in care is higher than it ever was.

In Ontario, First Nations children make up 2 percent of the population of children, but make up 10 percent of the children in care. In South Dakota, Native kids are 15 percent of the population, but make up 52 percent of the kids in care. In Alberta, 70 percent of the children in care are Indigenous, 55 percent in Alaska and 84 percent in Manitoba.

Many children are removed from homes affected by poverty or substance abuse, instead of providing families with the support and resources to raise their incomes or heal from addictions so that children can stay with their parents. Often poor housing is used as an excuse to take the kids. Many northern First Nations communities struggle in homes that are extremely crowded, have no indoor plumbing and are contaminated by mold. The children are taken instead of the homes being made safe.

Being taken into foster care is no guarantee of a better life for an Indigenous child. In six months of 2011 in Alberta alone, four Aboriginal kids died in foster care.

A class-action lawsuit is trying to hold the Canadian government accountable for the way First Nations children were damaged during the Sixties Scoop. The Indian Child Welfare Act in the United States gives tribes legal authority to have a voice in what happens to the children in their communities, although they don't always have the resources to be able to properly use that authority. And attention is being paid to keeping better records to make it easier for children who are taken to one day be able to find their way back home.

I've lived in the North Bay area since I was seven. Before that I lived in Moosonee on the shore of James Bay. My parents liked to move a lot. I am Cree.

I don't live with my parents now. My father is in North Bay. My mother moved to Kapuskasing.

The chaos started when I was five. I don't know exactly what went on. I remember my parents fighting a lot. My little sister Raya had just been born and I'd take care of her a lot, rocking her and protecting her when the fighting got bad.

We got put in our first foster home, but it was not a good place. One of the adults was a pervert. He did things to me that I didn't understand, and when I asked my mom about it, she complained to Children's Aid. He got caught and we got moved to a new foster home.

Mom and Dad got themselves straightened out, got us back and moved us back up to Moosonee for a while. My little brother was born there. Then we moved back to North Bay, and my little sister Kiyana was born.

My parents started fighting again. All my siblings would hide in my room. I was scared too, but I tried not to show it. I gave them games to keep their minds off the yelling and crashing. One time my mother made me run out into the street to find the cops because my dad was out of control.

We got sent to another foster home in another town, then got split up into different foster homes in North Bay.

After a while, our dad got stable and we were able to live with him. Then he had a stroke and we were sent back into foster care.

I think his stroke was brought on by stress. My little sister Kiyana was diagnosed with transverse myelitis, a disease of the spine. She was flown to the hospital in Ottawa with only a 50 percent chance of surviving. She pulled through, but she was paralyzed. The doctors said she'd never walk again, but she proved them wrong. She can walk and run now, but her hands claw up when she's at rest. We look exactly alike. She's ten now.

When Dad recovered, we went back to live with him, then things got out of hand again and it was back to foster care.

One of the foster families I got put with treated me really great, like I was one of them. They took me to Disney World and Universal Studios. I saw the real Jaws!

Then at long last we all got put with my mother, all four of us. For about six months everything was great. I had a long walk to school each day — about an hour each way — but I didn't mind.

I kept getting sore throats. They thought it was tonsillitis, then strep throat. Over and over it was happening. I constantly felt sick.

I came home from school one day to learn that black mold was in the house right where I was sleeping. We were given an hour to pack up and get out. Black mold is dangerous. We were taken to a crisis center and stayed there for a couple of months. The people who ran the center were nice, but it's not the sort of place where you can have a normal family life.

The day finally came when my tonsils were supposed to come out. I went into the hospital and on the same day my sister was in an accident on her bike and crashed her skull. She was put into another hospital and my mother went frantically between the two. I had an allergic reaction to the anesthetic, which delayed my recovery.

We went back to the crisis center and I started the new school year.

We finally left the crisis center and moved to a new house in the suburbs at the far end of North Bay. I was lonely. I don't make new friends easily, but I was glad to be out of the center. That is until there was a big drug bust across the street and we realized what a bad neighborhood we were in. There was violence all around us. One of my brothers was badly beaten up by some of the guys.

It got worse when my mom and her white boyfriend started dealing drugs out of our house. I think it was cocaine maybe, but I'm not sure. There would be all this money around that I knew was not supposed to be there.

All this stress made my grades slip. My teacher kept going at me to get my grades up. She had no idea about my life.

Around this time it came out that my brother Skyler had been badly abused by his foster mother. Constant hitting, slapping, punching and pushing. His foster dad had no idea this was happening. The foster dad was a good guy and was devastated when it all came out.

My mother was really angry about it. She was going to sue Children's Aid, but she started doing the drugs she was dealing and that made her fall apart. When she went into withdrawal she got very foul and angry and took it out on us. One time she was going after my sister. I told her to stop, and Mom threw me out of the house. I had no shoes on and the weather was bad. I had to walk a very long way to get to a friend's house.

The police came, and then it was off to another foster home. Then back with Mom and her boyfriend.

I started high school, a Catholic school where we wore uniforms. I went home from school one day to see the police outside my house. The house had been trashed — broken plates, drug needles everywhere, busted lightbulbs. A real mess. I didn't see much because the police wouldn't let me. They wouldn't even let me change out of my school uniform. So I was wearing the uniform when they took me to the hospital where my mom was in the emergency room.

She was all beaten up, black eyes, swollen all over.

She said the police were taking her boyfriend's side because he was white.

Then, of course, we got taken away to another foster home. We were split up again too.

I was sent to a really strict foster home. I wasn't used to having rules and I was not in good emotional shape. I asked to be moved to a home I'd feel more comfortable in. The worker kept promising but nothing would happen. Finally I took a bunch of Tylenol. Not enough to die. Just enough to wake up my worker. After I got out of emergency, they found me a new home. A good one. With really great people.

My grades went up. I got sent to a new foster home with a single woman heading it, and this one was good too.

One weekend a month, I'd get sent to a relief home. This is a place for teens who are hard to place — dropouts and runaways and kids with challenges. We'd go there to give our foster parents a weekend off. The relief home staff were always glad to see me because I'd be quiet and always did my chores.

My younger siblings all got adopted together. I was too old to be adopted, but I'm glad they have a proper home now, with good people.

Moving around so much is really hard. Every new foster home has rules you have to learn — both spoken and unspoken. I'd get very angry, but I'd try not to show it because I wouldn't want the foster parents to get a bad impression of me. I'd often have to change to a new school when I got a new foster home. After a while I stopped even trying to make friends.

My workers changed all the time too. I'd have to keep explaining my life to a new person, over and over.

Every time I got taken away from my parents, or from one foster home to another, I'd leave empty-handed. Just the clothes on my back. I'd get these comfort bags from the Children's Aid — a little bag with pajamas, a change of underwear, stuff like that.

I don't get attached to things. I don't get attached to people either. My younger siblings can say I love you, but I can't.

But for all that, I'm doing okay. I'm in a First Nations high school, and I'll be able to graduate. We learn traditional things as well as academic things. It helps me feel calm and grounded.

My plan is to go into nursing and then earn enough money to go to med school. I like science and I like helping people. It's my life now. Finally. My life is mine.

Abigail, 16

Four percent of Canada's Indigenous people identify themselves as Inuit, a word that means People. Inuit have lived in the high Arctic for more than four thousand years, creating their lives in harsh climates — hunting, fishing and building homes from materials they had on hand.

Nunavut makes up one-fifth of the nation of Canada. It is home to 80 percent of Inuit. Many live in overcrowded, substandard conditions, with global warming and mineral exploration making their traditional hunting and fishing nearly impossible.

There are also communities in the southern part of Canada, primarily in Winnipeg and Ottawa.

I met with Abigail and her friends at the Ottawa Inuit Children's Centre.

My mother was born on the land in Pangnirtung, Nunavut. It's on Baffin Island, north of Iqaluit. It's almost 100 percent Inuit. Very few white people there. Inuit have lived there for more than a thousand years.

My father was born in Orillia. His background is Scottish and Irish. I've always lived in Ottawa.

My niece Thai comes to this center too. She's my niece even though she's only one year younger. Her father was born in China.

Thai and two of her brothers live with me and my family now. She was put into a foster home when she was young, then went back to her parents, but it wasn't safe for her there, so my parents took the three of them in. One of her other brothers and one of her sisters were adopted into Inuit families. Two of her sisters still live with her mom and stepfather in Pangnirtung.

It sounds really confusing, but the bottom line is that Thai and her brothers live with me and my family. It's by the grace of God, really. They could have been split up and sent to foster homes all around Canada.

I visited Pangnirtung a few summers ago and had a bit of culture shock. I'm used to living in the big city with many things going on. Pangnirtung is very small — maybe 1,500 people — and at first I felt kind of stranded. Behind the town is the mountains and in front of the town is the bay that leads to the ocean. And that's it. Once you're there, you're there. In Ottawa, if I feel like leaving the city, I know I can hop on a train or a bus and go to Kingston or Montreal or Toronto. But in Pangnirtung there are no roads out of town. You're just there.

But once I got over that feeling, I really loved it. You can't believe how beautiful it is. The mountains are amazing. Beluga whales come into the bay to have their babies. You can spot seals and sometimes walruses.

As for the town, well, there's a community center with a museum and a library and a place for elders to go. There's a church, a Northern store that sells groceries and things, arts and crafts shops, a co-op, a hotel and that's about it.

I was there during the summer. There was 24-hour sunlight. I had to put garbage bags over the windows to be able to get to sleep. There were all these kids playing outside at one in the morning, having a great time.

I loved walking in the mountains with my sister and mom. It's the freshest air up there! And you can see for such a long way. You can see the whole community. There's water trickling down the mountains into pools. It's cold, fresh and clean. Everyone loves you up there. You're family.

I loved playing with the kids in the community. We played Inuit baseball. That's baseball without any rules! We went clam digging at low tide out in the ocean. If you find one it splashes water on your face. It was so exciting to find a jellyfish. My brother Mark caught an Arctic char. We went to the gym and played volleyball. Lots of great things.

But there were some not great things too.

My Uncle Michael was drunk a lot. It's like he has to have alcohol. It's very sad and it's hard to be around. I felt like I was walking on eggshells around him. You never know what's going on in the head of someone who's drinking. I know I was safe because I was with Mom and Gran, but I still didn't like it.

We went to church up there on Sunday mornings. The first one we went to was in the old Anglican style, reading from a book. The second one we went to was more alive — kids playing guitar, rejoicing. It was a really happy service and I loved being there.

I'd like to live up there for a while. I'd also like to be able to speak fluent Inuktitut. The language is disappearing fast. Some parents and elders and teachers are trying to keep it alive. It must be difficult for the Inuit who've always lived up there in all the quiet and beauty when they come to Ottawa where it's noisy and busy.

All my friends in Ottawa think it's really cool that I'm Inuit. My ancestors were the first people here and that gives me a huge sense of honor. Other Inuit kids I know have had people make fun of them. Some people mistake us for Mexican or Filipino or Chinese. And when I say I'm Inuit, they say, "What's that?" It's kind of funny. I feel sorry for them because they know so little.

The Inuit center is terrific because they have so much going on — daycare, language classes, camps. You can do art, fitness, hip-hop. Later today we're going on a field trip to visit other Inuit groups here in Ottawa. I think that will be good. Canadian stuff is all around here — the parliament buildings, the war museum, the prime minister's house — and that's great and easy for us to see. It will be good to meet the other Inuit groups because they're harder to find than the parliament buildings, and we might want to join them when we're older. And we'll talk about the center to them so we'll get experience in talking out in front of strangers.

I don't know yet what I want to be when I get older. I love art, singing and basketball. I also love little kids. And I feel called in my life to do something for the church, doing some reaching out to other people around the world, maybe volunteering in overseas missions, or helping people with addictions and mental illness.

I've had a really good upbringing. I've been very lucky.

The Ottawa Inuit Children's Centre (www.ottawainuitchildrens.com) works with parents and the community to foster strong and proud Inuit children, youth and families.

Cohen, 14

Off the northern British Columbia coast sit the islands of Haida Gwaii. The Haida people have occupied them for more than eight thousand years, eating off the land and the ocean, using cedars for homes and canoes and creating incredible works of art. Because the islands are so remote, the Europeans were slow to arrive. Still, from a society of more than 120 villages, by 1911 there were only 589 Haida left, clinging together in two villages.

Under Haida tradition, a person held in high esteem is not someone who has the most but someone who gives away the most. One of the big ceremonies for doing this is the potlatch — a feast at which the host gives things away.

Missionaries of the day were part of the driving force behind the 1884 amendment to the Indian Act (as well as a similar act in the United States) that made the potlatch illegal, calling for the imprisonment of anyone who organized or encouraged participation in the potlatch. That law was not repealed until 1951.

I met Cohen and his friends in a community center in Haida Gwaii.

Haida Gwaii is a real peaceful place. There's forest, clean water, ocean. If storms happen and the ferry doesn't come, we still have plenty of food. We just go outside and harvest it ourselves. My favorite food is k'aaw, which is herring eggs on kelp. There's steelhead in the rivers. They're a very fast fish. There are clams to dig. There's even octopus.

Octopus hunting is fun. You look for a rock that has a lot of crab shells around it. That tells you the octopus has been eating there. You use a trap that looks like a tube, then you use a hose to blow air under the rock to get the octopus out of its hiding place.

Octopus is called naaw in Haida. It tastes creamy on the inside. It tastes a little like clams, actually. It's rubbery on the outside.

There's crabs to eat, sea cucumbers, sea urchins. With sea urchins you peel away the red spiny parts and eat the inside. It's really salty.

We gather chanterelle mushrooms. You have to know what you're doing because if you pick the wrong kind of mushrooms you have to dump them out and all your work will be wasted. You fry the mushrooms, but you dry them first.

Our whole class goes out to the beach to gather seaweed. It has to be black with just a hint of deep green, and you pick it off a rock.

The food here is clean. We can just go outside, find it and eat it. It's not damaged by pollution. There was this great blackberry bush with huge blackberries on it, but someone accidentally dumped some oil on it, and it got contaminated. But other than that it's all clean.

On the island here it's not so much about money, because nobody really has any. It's about family and community. You know everyone on the rock. Our parents know everything that goes on with us. We don't have a problem with secrets. People here look after each other. There's always an open door. If you really don't want to be at home, someone will take you in.

You can't steal a car here because you know everyone's car, and so does everyone else, and everyone knows you. Drugs and alcohol are here, sure, but they're everywhere. I think it isn't such a problem among the Haida because we're able to keep so close to our traditions, and to practice the traditions you have to be drug and alcohol free.

My chanii [grandfather] and my nana and others ran away from the residential school they were put into. Some of the older generation like my great-grandparents looked at the residential school as a good thing, but the schools weren't as bad for them. For my nana and chanii, it was a whole lot of abuse. They were treated really badly.

My Haida teacher said we Haida are lucky. Our island is so remote that we didn't have to deal with white invaders for as long as other First Nations did. When the whites came, though, they were mean. The teacher told us about what went on at those schools, and about the Truth and Reconcilation Commission. How do people ever heal from that experience?

My mother works with residential school survivors. Prime Minister Stephen Harper has apologized, and I guess we have to accept it. I don't know. If we had done the same to whites, would the whites forgive us if we said I'm sorry?

My mother says there is no way to make up for the crimes of the past. There's only forward.

The residential schools are only part of it. The Canadian government in the past made a lot of our ceremonies and sa-

Haida Gwaii.

cred things illegal. Like the potlatch. Our way of conducting business is to give gifts. When you accept the gift or eat the food provided at a feast, you are honoring the person who gives them. The acceptance is part of it. It's not I'm giving you gifts to prove I'm richer and more powerful than you. It's more I honor you by giving and you honor me by receiving.

Some potlatches can have hundreds of people. You can imagine the work. It brings the community together. All the food has to be caught and prepared. Usually there's a seafood soup or a venison stew and buns, then k'aaw or crab, and berries. The food is served on long tables decorated with cedar boughs.

At a potlatch there's always a witnessing. A blanket is sewn to honor someone and the community witnesses the honor. Then the honored person has to validate the blanket by dancing in it.

People give gifts to mark the death of a family member too. A year after you die you have a headstone raising. There has to be a ceremony at the cemetery where you clean the stone and then there's a feast, and the family gives gifts to everyone there.

At the feast and headstone raising of a chief, his family gave away cloth bags with his name on it. Inside was a chocolate bar in the shape of the chief's headgear. They'd had it made at a factory in Vancouver. Another elder who passed loved the color purple, and his family gave away gifts with a purple theme.

A few years ago some logging companies tried to come onto our land on Lyell Island. They got permits to cut down the trees, but they didn't get permission from us, and we didn't want them there. There were lots of protests and lots of people were arrested.

My dad was part of the stand-off. A lot of our parents were. My mom, my uncles. Everyone was. There were a lot of elders getting arrested and some of them went to trial. It was before my time. The Haida won, and Gwaii Haanas National Park was created.

This is very old land. In Gwaii Haanas, the south island, people are still finding totem poles and canoes that were carved hundreds and hundreds of years ago, covered up by moss and forest that's grown over them.

A lot of us go hunting, especially for deer. There's lots of deer. They're a good food source. You can really tell the difference in taste between a deer you shoot and meat you buy in a store. We all grew up skinning and gutting deer and other animals. It's not gross to us. It's a skill. It's food.

It wouldn't be that hard for me — or any of us — to live now as we lived four hundred years ago. We're already used to living off the land. We know — or, our elders know — how to use plants and animals to keep warm and dry. I know we could totally do it.

It was our belief that the love of possessions is a weakness to be overcome. Its appeal is to the material part, and if allowed its way, it will in time disturb the spiritual balance of the man. Therefore the child must early learn the beauty of generosity. He is taught to give what he prizes most, and that he may taste the happiness of giving.

— Ohiyesa (Charles Alexander Eastman), Wahpeton Santee Sioux

Miranda, 12

According to a 2011 study by the World Health Organization, the small community of Sarnia, Ontario, has the worst air quality in all of Canada. Just outside the town is Chemical Valley, an area of massive factories that belong to Canada's petrochemical industry.

Directly beside the factories is the First Nations community of Aamjiwnaang. One side of the reserve sits right beside Sarnia. On another side is the St. Clair River, a dividing line between Ontario and Michigan. Chemical Valley makes up the third line of this triangle. A wire fence separates the factories from the reserve's daycare center.

Miranda is the daughter of the Aamjiwnaang First Nation chief. I met her in her school.

I love living on the reserve. It's fun. There are lots of community events. I have friends here.

Dad was elected chief. He likes being chief and takes it seriously. He goes to a lot of meetings. He takes care of things. People bring him their problems and he tries to fix them. He still manages to leave it all at work so that when he comes home he's just a dad. Most of the time.

Mom is a daycare teacher on the reserve. I'd like to do that

Chemical Valley.

too. Sometimes I go there to help out. They do special craft workshops I help with, like basketmaking at Easter.

I'm okay at baskets. I'm better at beading.

The hardest thing about living on this reserve is that there are a whole lot of petrochemical plants right on the edge of our land. DuPont, Shell, Dow. Lots of others.

There's just a regular wire fence separating our land from the factories. We'll see the chemical guys walking around in special protective clothes. And just across the wire the reserve kids are playing in the grass. Sometimes the air is hard to breathe. It hurts my throat. Lots of people have coughs that never go away.

The companies all say it's safe, that there's no pollution, but we can't even go wading in some of our streams now because of all the chemicals.

Sometimes there's a spill from one of the factories and

they call Dad. He has to alert everyone to get inside their homes and stay there until it's safe to go outside again.

We are surrounded by the factories. I sometimes think they would like it if we all died in a chemical spill. Then they could take over our land and fill it with more factories. Like all those people they killed in India.

Sign on the edge of Miranda's reserve.

There are sirens all over the area that are supposed to go off when there's a spill, but they don't always work. They test them every Monday at 12:30. There's a daycare center and a place for seniors on the reserve right by the factories, and often the sirens there don't work.

One time there was a spill and everyone in Corunna [a small community just south of Sarnia] was evacuated, but not the reserve, even though it's closer.

It's almost a normal thing here to die of cancer, especially if you're a woman. Lots of women here have it, and they don't even have to be old. Even in their thirties they get it. Thirty is old, but it's not really old. Women have a lot of miscarriages too.

We used to swim in the river. There were no warnings posted, so we just did it. We'd come out of the water with big gobs of tar stuck all over us. No wonder the fish and the frogs are all being born with, like, three eyes and weird bodies. We probably all glow in the dark. Fish have tumors and kittens and puppies are born all deformed.

Then there's the pollution from people being idiots. Boats are not allowed to dump their crap into the river, but big private pleasure boats — owned by whites, of course — will come into our territory to dump their waste because they figure it doesn't matter, they won't get caught. My friends and I run down to the dock and yell at them. We shame them and make them go away. It's a bit of a victory, but why do rich people have to be morons?

If I had all the power in the universe I'd take away the chemical plants, make the reserve a bit bigger and have everything clean and good again. My ancestors used to be able to drink from the river. Imagine that! When they got thirsty they could just go down to the river, scoop up some water and drink it.

I would like to be able to do that again.

Our village was healthy and there was no place in the country possessing such advantage, nor no hunting grounds better than those we had in possession. If another prophet had come to our village in those days and told us what has since taken place, none of our people would have believed him.

— Ma-ka-tai-me-she-kia-kiak, or Black Hawk, Chief of the Sauk and Fox Tribe

Jeremy, 16

First Nations children with disabilities can face extra challenges, from the remoteness of their communities, the lack of resources available to them, and racism that too often goes hand in hand with the providing of health and social services.

Contrary to the commonly accepted belief that there are way more First Nations children with Fetal Alcohol Spectrum Disorder (brain damage occurring in an unborn baby when a pregnant woman drinks alcohol) than in other communities, some studies say the numbers are the same. What's different is that if a First Nations child has challenges, she is more likely to be labeled with FASD automatically, with other causes such as autism or environmental pollution not even considered or tested for. The wrong diagnosis means the child does not get the proper treatment.

Jeremy is Mi'kmaq and a member of Pictou Landing First Nation in Nova Scotia. His ancestors have been in this territory for more than 9,000 years. There are thirty-five reserves today in Nova Scotia, with a population of about 25,000 people.

I spoke with Jeremy's mother about her son.

Before giving birth to Jeremy, his mother, Maurina, spent five years in Sarnia, in Chemical Valley. She thinks Jeremy may have been affected by all the chemical factories in the area. He was born hydrocephalic, which means there was liquid on his brain. He has since also been diagnosed with cerebral palsy and autism.

When they presented Jeremy to his mother, they told her he probably wasn't going to live long. His mom looked down at him and said, "It's you and me against the world, baby. You and I are gonna work real hard."

She gave him the best care she could, with special massages and exercises for his eyes. She took him with her everywhere so he wouldn't feel like a stranger in the world. Between hospital stays, he would go to school, where the kids liked him and treated him well.

His first school was mixed, for white and Native kids. Jeremy enjoyed being there. But he would sometimes bang his head — maybe because he was frustrated or because the shunt in his head caused him pain. To try to get him to stop, the staff put him in a small room and turned out the lights. A staff member said Jeremy had been in the room like that for just a few minutes. Kids at the school told Jeremy's mother it had been more like an hour.

The Pictou Landing First Nation told Jeremy's mother she could bring him there. And she did.

For many years workers came to her home to help her with Jeremy. Jeremy needs a lot of care, as there are many things he can't do on his own. He gets high fevers and at times he starts gagging and can't get himself to stop. He gets pneumonia easily and often.

A little while ago his mother had a stroke. It has become very hard for her to look after Jeremy. And the money that Pictou Landing First Nation has to hire helpers is running out. His mother doesn't know what to do.

The federal government told her that if she took him off the reserve and put him in an institution, they would pay for his care. But there was no separate funding for children with disabilities who live on reserves.

His mother doesn't want to put him in an institution. On the reserve he has friends, people talk to him. One friend comes over and tells him, "Get your shoes, it's time for a cruise!" And Jeremy laughs and gets excited. If he's put into an institution, his mother is afraid he'll become a lonely guy, lost inside himself.

Then his mother discovered Jordan's Principle, named after Jordan River Anderson of the Norway House Cree Nation. Jordan spent the entire four years of his life in the hospital while different levels of government argued about who would pay for him to be cared for at his home. The principle declares that the needs of a First Nations child should be met first, and any intergovernmental squabbling about payment should happen after.

Now she has another way to fight.

"Jeremy is a wonderful little man," she says. "He loves to go to the beach. He doesn't swim, but he can walk around in the water. Water is heavy and it makes his legs stronger. He likes watching the PBS station on TV, and he likes listening to music. He can use his feet like they are a second pair of hands. He's a wonderful son. When people take the time to know him, they always like him."

Larry, 18

For many years, silence surrounded residential school
survivors. The people who
had committed unspeak-
able crimes against these
children went on with their
lives and careers, not having to account for what they
had done. The governments
and institutions that had for-
mulated the policies to create and manage the residential school system went on to create new policies.
They did not look back at the destruction they had
caused until the survivors, with great courage, started
speaking out and demanding better.

In Canada, the Truth and Reconciliation Commission was established to provide a forum for survivors
of residential schools to tell their stories as well as
have them recorded and acknowledged. Communities are using traditional ceremonies to help survivors
and their descendants heal from the experience. Mohawk women of the Six Nations use traditional griev-
ing rituals with songs and prayers to help release
people from the trauma they have been through. The
Weeneebayko Area Health Authority assists communities in the James Bay area of northern Ontario
through traditional Cree ceremonies like shaking
tents. The Aboriginal Healing Foundation, whose
funding was discontinued by the federal government

in 2010, provided assistance to many communities seeking to heal from what happened to them.

Religious institutions and governments have paid compensation to the victims of abuse at their schools. The Canadian prime minister gave an official apology in 2008, and residential school survivors are paid tribute to in a stained-glass window at the House of Commons.

The silence and shame that surrounded this experience have started to be lifted, and people are reclaiming their heritage and their pride.

Larry lives in South Indian Lake in northern Manitoba. He is about to graduate from high school.

Mom and Dad both got to grade nine. My dad works for hydro now. My mom died of alcohol poisoning a couple of years ago. I think she had her share of problems when she was young. She tried her best to keep us happy. She made sure we had clothes, made sure we ate. She was a really good mom. I miss her a lot. She taught me how to be a good person.

My parents were always fighting. They were on the verge of separating when she died.

I have five brothers and five sisters. I'm the second youngest. My older brother Lorne killed himself in 2007. We grew up seeing drugs and alcohol around all the time. Mom would try to hide it all from us and keep it quiet, but kids always know what's going on. I looked after my younger brother. The older kids looked after the both of us.

My grandparents are residential school survivors. My grandpa lasted until grade ten. He sometimes talks about it. The terrible ways they got disciplined. He had to put his hand flat on his desk and leave it there while the teacher hit him over and over with a ruler. If he pulled his hand back, he got hit more.

South Indian Lake is a nine-hour bus ride from this school. I go home only for Christmas and spring break unless the weather is too bad. I'm at school most of the year.

South Indian Lake is small. It's a Cree community. Some of the elders still speak Cree fluently, which is a miracle when you think of everything that happened to them at the residential school. There's moose, caribou, bears, some houses, a school, a fire hall, a Northern store, a health complex. There used to be a pool hall, but it burned down.

There are a lot of traditional practices in the community. One of them is youth drumming practice. I've gone with my cousins. You learn to play with a good rhythm and to do the proper preparation before you play. You smudge with sweetgrass to cleanse, then you present an offering of tobacco to honor the drum. We drum at community gatherings and events like Treaty Days and Games Days. It makes me feel proud to be learning something that's been passed down for generations.

My Uncle Frank is trying to get someone to teach Hoop dancing. It would be pretty awesome to see some kids from our community doing Hoop dancing.

Our community used to be on one side of the lake but then a dam was built and the community was flooded out and got moved to higher ground. People's memories were washed away. The water used to be clear. Now it's all muddy. It used to be healthy with fish, but there are hardly any fish now. My people got had.

The homes in the community are very crowded. In my house there are twelve people — me, my brother, my sister Thelma, Thelma's boyfriend, my sister Dorothy, Thelma's kids Josh Jr., Kathy, Lorne, Jermine, Dorothy's kids Shawn and Wayne, and my friend Marty, whose parents drink so he came to see if he could stay with us. It's a small house. People sleep everywhere.

So many of us are in there, but it makes it easy to watch the kids. There's always someone around to keep an eye on them. It all somehow works out.

When I was eleven I was taken away by Child and Family Services. They put me in a foster home in Thompson. I was there for a year and a half. The people were nice to me but I was missing home so much. For the longest time I didn't talk at all or watch TV or eat hardly anything. I stayed in bed for a long time with the covers over my head. My sister was in the same foster home. She kept telling me everything was going to be all right, that Mom would come and get us.

Then we went back to our parents. They'd drink after we went to bed. We'd get up early and clean the house before we went to school. You could smell the booze in the air.

Dad still drinks large amounts of alcohol whenever he gets the chance. He's had two minor strokes and his heart is weak. I ask him to stop but ...

He goes out to Nelson House for work. He's gone for months, comes back for a bit, then goes off again.

I try to be a good person. Sometimes I have turned to drugs and alcohol. Then I would see this chain. My grandparents drank and my parents drank and all this pain is like a chain around our community. Sometimes I find it hard to walk around my community without running into a drunk. I ask them, "Why are you hurting yourself?" They say, "I want to forget." I try to tell them alcohol isn't the answer.

It's supposed to be a dry community, but bootleggers smuggle it in. It's very frustrating. I try to keep it out of my house. I look after my nieces and nephews and keep the house clean.

There are big problems, but small bits of light can help. The people in South Indian Lake are good people. Even with all the pain they try to be there for each other. I'm proud to be a part of them.

I've been to Winnipeg a couple of times. It may have everything but it doesn't have that feeling of earth. Everything is covered in concrete.

I wish I'd lived five hundred years ago, back when there was no arrival of white men. I think it would be easier. Just hunt and fish to provide for your family and live. And I'd be speaking my own language, which I'm still trying to do.

I guess I'm hopeful though. I don't want my kids growing up seeing me drunk and covered in mud. I've thought about it for a very long time, whether I can make a difference so that none of this alcohol or drugs will be here. It's a sickness and I'm just wanting to try to get it away. A lot of people feel the way I do.

Human beings are all the same. White people have their share of problems too.

Destiny, 15

The Pine Ridge Indian Reservation in South Dakota was known as the Great Sioux Reservation when it was created by the Treaty of Fort Laramie in 1851. It was originally more than 60 million acres in size. After homesteaders and gold-rushers moved in, the American government reduced the reservation's size in 1868. It is now 2.8 million acres, around the same size as the state of Connecticut.

It is home to 38,000 citizens of the Oglala Band of Lakota Sioux. It is also one of the most poverty-stricken places in the United States. With high rates of diabetes, tuberculosis, alcoholism and suicide, it has one of the lowest life-expectancy rates in the Western Hemisphere.

It is also a place full of people who are working really hard to make things better. Small businesses are growing, from crafts to restaurants to shops for hikers and campers. Community members are exploring green technologies and Band-run public transit. Sioux-Preme Wood Products is a new business that makes affordable, beautiful caskets lined with Native blankets and carved with traditional designs. With support from Lakota Funds and South Dakota State University, gardeners are being trained to grow and market fresh vegetables to the community. And the community recently opened up its first movie theater.

Young people on Pine Ridge are finding new ways to express themselves. Five young runners went to New York City in 2012 to run the marathon and ended up volunteering to help with the clean-up after Hurricane Sandy. Others are using different media to break through stereotypes others have about them.

Destiny is a tenth grader who lives in the village of Porcupine on the Pine Ridge reservation. She and her schoolmates have made videos about their lives.

I'm a full-blooded Native American, part of the Lakota Nation. My family has been in Pine Ridge forever. My father works at the Pine Ridge jail and my mother works for the Department of Public Safety. It's nice here, pretty quiet, lots of plains, some trees here and there. There are a lot of deer, bobcats, wolves, mountain lions. You have to respect them. My parents don't like me to go out alone at night because of the animals.

My family is very traditional and practices a lot of the old ways. I take part in powwows as a dancer. My dad's mother teaches me to cook and clean and tells me to keep my hair long. If a close member of my family dies, then I will cut my hair as a sign of mourning. I'm saving my hair for when my grandmother passes away.

I was part of a film called *Reservation Realities*.

The whole thing was a great experience. I love writing. I loved working on the acting. I played the part of a kid in a family that tried to look like it is a perfect family only it isn't so perfect. The parents fight in front of the kids and there's a lot of tension and hard times. A girl named Trinity Bald Eagle had the idea. We all talked about it and formed it into a story.

Nobody asks children what they go through and how they feel about it. Adults look at kids and go, Oh, I wish I was young like that and didn't have any worries, or, Oh, that kid is such a pain. I wish they would go away. But they don't really listen to us.

But we have problems just like adults. My older brothers and sisters have problems with alcohol, although they never drink around the house. They keep it away from the rest of us, which I appreciate. My mother quit drinking when she decided to start having babies. My dad also quit before I was born, so I've been brought up with good sober parents.

I tried drinking booze a couple of times with my older brothers. I thought it was a big waste of time. It's not going to be a part of my life. I see what it does. It's not good.

There's a lot of suicide around here. Kids my age and even younger than me. I think it's because it's so hard for most kids to find someone to talk to. We have a mental health agency at the hospital but kids aren't going to go there on their own. People find out you go there and it's like, Oh, you're weird!

My friend Tea killed herself before she finished eighth grade.

She was very athletic. She was friendly, loving, caring, interested in what was going on. She was always wanting to make new friends and get to know people.

I don't know why she killed herself. I didn't know her family situation, but I know that kids can have the greatest family there is and still feel like they're all alone.

How I found out about it was I was texting her ex-boyfriend and he told me that Tea had killed herself.

I was like, No!

And he texted, I'm not lying! She did it!

I didn't want to believe him, so I got hold of her cousin and found out for sure that it was true.

I went to her funeral and saw her in her casket. She was only fourteen. She shouldn't have been in a casket. They had a lot of pictures of her at the funeral. She was just a kid!

And I'll never get to see her again.

My niece tried to kill herself a lot of times. I tried too, but only three times. I think I'm a bit stronger than my niece.

The first time I tried to kill myself I was thirteen. After it didn't work, I told my parents about it. They were too shocked and sad at first to really react much, and I thought that meant that they didn't care. But later I came to know that they did care and still do.

I cut my throat three times but nothing happened. I OD'd on sleeping pills and I tried to hang myself. Nothing worked. I stayed alive.

I've been given a whole bunch of second chances. I guess I was meant to live. I guess maybe the Creator is telling me to hang on, it's going to be okay, you've got something important to do before you die, so just ride out the hard stuff.

There's not a lot to do out here to relax when you're feeling stress. When I lived down the road from my grandmother's, I would go to the basketball court and monkey bars that were in the neighborhood. Now we've moved. It's just a small housing area, nothing but plains around. I go for a lot of long walks. That helps.

I haven't had a lot of contact with white people, and most of what I've had hasn't been all that good. I go to Rapid City sometimes. A lot of Natives live there too. White kids have yelled things, calling us ghetto. White adults call us Wagon Burners, Squaws. I'm not a violent person. I look at them when they say things and then I just look away. I have no business with them.

I put it down to ignorance. White people are ignorant

about us because they never have to think about us. They don't know what we've been through ever since the settlers came.

I live just over the hill from where the Wounded Knee Massacre took place, over by Wounded Knee Creek. On December 29, 1890, the Seventh Cavalry rounded up two Lakota tribes, the Miniconjou and the Hunkpapa, and took them to the creek. They tried to take a rifle away from one of the elders, but he didn't want to give it up because it had cost him a lot of money. So the army started shooting and killed at least 150 Lakota Sioux. They killed women, children, old men. Just shot them. My cousin's great-great-grandfather was one of the survivors.

For white kids it's just something in a history book. For me it's my family. It's my ground that they bled on. It's personal.

They're still killing us today, but now they do it with alcohol and drugs and bad food and suicide.

When the whites killed all the buffalo, they left us without the main thing we used to eat. So by treaty they have to give us food. It's called commodity food — canned goods, canned vegetables, canned meats. We can't eat like we used to. A few people on the rez have full hunting licenses, but not many.

A lot of people have diabetes from bad food. My dad has it, so I'm more likely to get it. So I take care of myself. I keep my weight down. My parents don't bring junk food in the house and my mom always tells me to eat my vegetables.

There has been a lot of fighting over this land and a lot of people have died here. They're still dying here. We're a very hurting people, and nobody notices it unless we force them to.

Because of all that, and because I survived all those suicide attempts, I don't take my life for granted now. I'm not an angel. I skip school sometimes but mostly I study hard and make plans for the future. I enjoy building things in wood-shop at school — I built a shelf for the bathroom — and I really enjoy writing. I'd love to go to the New York Film Academy. I also wouldn't mind being a high-school math teacher. I'm involved in cheerleading and other school things. And Christmas is coming! My mother is very religious — both the Christian and the Lakota religion — and when we decorate, we have the brightest house on the butte.

I would not go so far as to say I'm optimistic about the future, but I won't let that get in the way of me being happy.

Reservation Realities can be seen on YouTube.

Isabella, 14

Over the decades, many Hollywood movies have depicted Indigenous people as wild, bloodthirsty savages who speak in grunts, or as helpful sidekicks who speak in one-syllable words. More substantial Indigenous roles would be played by non-Natives in make-up.

Indigenous filmmakers are now telling their own stories, penned by Indigenous writers and featuring Indigenous actors.

Isabella is a Dakota from Sisseton in South Dakota.

I live in St. Paul. I've always lived in the city. I have family on the reservation, and I visit there a lot.

The thing I really love to do is acting. I've been in a few plays with local theater companies. I feel very passionate about acting and theater and that whole performing world.

One of my recent roles was in the play *Jane Gibbs' Farm*. Jane Gibbs was a real girl who lived with her family on their farm and made friends with the Dakota people. I auditioned and got the part.

I was really nervous at the audition. I always am, at every audition. But I've been told that it's good to be nervous. It means you're on your toes.

I have so much fun at rehearsals! You start out not knowing your lines, not knowing your character or where you're supposed to be standing, and as rehearsals go on, it all settles in your head. It's hard work but it is so much fun!

Acting is about being able to create someone different from who I am. In my regular life, I'm pretty shy and quiet. You wouldn't think that a shy person would want to go up on a stage in front of a lot of people. But I don't act to get people to look at me. I act to explore new things and new people. Being onstage I can be so different from who I am regularly. And every character I portray rubs off on me somehow.

I was in a play two or three years ago by Rhiana Yazzie. It was called *Rainbow Crow*. It was a story about a crow that had beautiful colors. Then she goes on a journey and loses her colors. I portrayed a crow. It was difficult but fun. I was flying around the stage and had to do a lot of exercises so that my arms would be strong enough to keep up for the length of the performance. I had to learn how to move like a crow too.

I haven't had any formal theater training yet. One day I will — I really want to — but for now I'm happy learning as I go.

Right now I'm in a production of *The Emperor's New Clothes*. I'm playing one of the people that has to trick the emperor. We open soon. I have a little stage fright on opening night. After opening night, I'm more excited than nervous.

When I'm on stage I always know I'm acting, but I work really hard to be the character. But I can't disappear too much into the character because you have to pay attention when you're on stage. Someone may forget a line or something else might happen and you have to be able to just go with it and keep the play going.

I started acting when I was really young. My father was a Dakota interpreter at Fort Snelling. Fort Snelling used to be a military fort but now it's falling apart. The historical society wants to put a lot of money into fixing it. I worked there with my dad when I was six. We would dress and do things the Dakota would have done back in history.

Fort Snelling was basically a concentration camp for the Dakota people. It's on sacred land where these two rivers meet. Sixteen hundred Santee Sioux — mostly women, children and elders — were kept there in terrible conditions. That was when President Lincoln had thirty-eight Dakota men hanged. It was the largest execution in American history. My family members do a memorial run in their honor.

When I was younger I went to the American Indian Magnet School. It focused on Native culture. The school I'm in now has only a couple of Native kids. I don't exactly hide my heritage from everyone but I don't feel really comfortable sharing it either because I don't think they'll understand.

I've had times when white people didn't understand. They thought they did but they didn't. There was a time when we went on a school retreat at a camp in northern Minnesota. We had a class about the Ojibwe people. The Ojibwe have a lot of territory in Minnesota. The teacher wanted all us kids to make up an Indian name for ourselves and call each other by these Indian names for the whole retreat. It made me uncomfortable, all these white kids making up what they thought were Indian-sounding names — whatever that means — and I told the teacher I didn't want to do it. Naming ceremonies are sacred. They mean something. I don't think the teacher understood that.

My father was in foster care all his life. He went from foster home to foster home. He was never adopted. It's really affected him. It's hard for him to make connections with people. All that moving around. He says it makes kids feel disconnected from everyone and everything. He's had lots of pain.

My grandmother — Dad's mother — was sent to a residential school that she managed to run away from. He never met her. He was taken away from her when he was born, and then she died. He never knew his father. When Dad grew up, he reconnected with his mother's sister, and they became close.

Dad dealt with all his pain by becoming involved in the American Indian Movement — AIM. I grew up hearing all about it. I did a lot of research on it too, when I did a history project on it.

On the Trail of Broken Treaties march they went to the BIA [Bureau of Indian Affairs] headquarters in Washington to get decent housing for elders but the riot police came and started beating people, so AIM kicked everyone out and occupied the building, just took it over. For six days they were there.

Dad was part of the Longest Walk. In 1978 they walked from California to Washington, DC, and set up a tepee on the lawn of the White House.

There's a picture of Dad and my uncle and another AIM member after they took over the BIA, standing on a car, looking at the FBI building.

I'm really proud of my father. I want to be someone who stands up like that.

We have all these racist Native mascots in the United States. They've used Native names for sports teams — baseball, football — like the Redskins and the Blackhawks. I've had white people tell me, "You shouldn't be upset by that. We're celebrating you!" But people are not mascots. You can't oppress us and steal from us then expect us to be grateful. All the Native people I know hate that these names are used.

If the whites really want to honor us they should fund our schools.

So I have lots going on in my life. I love acting, and maybe that's how I'll serve our people. We'll just have to wait and see!

Danton, 14

The Canadian nation began with the fur trade. Beaver hats were all the rage in Europe and there was money to be made. The Hudson's Bay Company controlled this trade, and the European men brought over to work for the company fathered children with Aboriginal women. Their descendants are known as Métis. The Métis culture is distinctly different from First Nations culture, although with many shared points in history. Like First Nations, many Métis were forced into residential schools.

Danton is Métis. He plays with the Métis Fiddler Quartet. Their debut album, *North West Voyage Nord Ouest*, won the 2012 Canadian Folk Music Award for Traditional Album of the Year.

I am Métis. In Canada, that's a blend of Aboriginal and European. We have a very distinct culture with our own music and traditions. We came about when the French invaded Iroquois territory way back in the days of the fur trade. They say the first Métis appeared nine months after the first Frenchman landed! For a better definition, look it up in the Canadian constitution. It's all spelled out in there.

We were not included in the original treaties the government of Canada made with the First Nations. We had to live off-reserve and were not really accepted by either culture. So we created our own.

I play music in a family group called the Métis Fiddler Quartet. I have two older brothers and an older sister. We tour around and play music at festivals and all kinds of events.

I play the cello. My sister chose the cello for me when I was a baby. The family group already had fiddlers and guitar players. She said, "We need a cello." So I learned. It's great.

I started playing when I was three. When you're that small you start with a viola or a small cello. I love the sound the cello makes. Mostly I'm a classical musician. I also play piano, guitar and bass guitar. It's fun to monkey around with different styles and instruments.

Although I do a lot of things that are not specifically Métis, like gymnastics, science, jazz, swimming and reading, being Métis is a big part of me. My Métis heritage is something I'm really proud of.

I'm related to Louis Riel way, way back. His grandmother was my great-great, like seven greats grandmother.

Louis Riel was a Métis leader who was hanged by the Canadian government for being a traitor, but really he was a hero.

It was in 1885. The Métis of Saskatchewan and Manitoba tried for a long time to get the Canadian government to acknowledge their rights to the land, but the government kept ignoring them. So they set up their own government. Louis Riel was their leader.

Things started to happen. Some soldiers got killed in Duck Lake. So the Canadian government got an army together to deal with the misbehaving Métis. And Louis Riel was hanged for treason.

We sing that history every time we perform. I feel it, probably because we have studied with some of the elders of Métis music, like Lawrence "Teddy Boy" Houle and James Flett. They showed us tunes, told us stories. Because of people like them, we know our history and can be proud of it.

It wasn't so easy for my grandmother, my mother's mother. She lived in a little French community in Manitoba and they were really poor. After the Métis rebellion was crushed, the government redistributed Métis land and the Métis got the less fertile bits. So generations had to deal with poverty. Then the government put Métis children into residential schools and you've heard about what a mess that was.

When my grandmother was a child it was against the law for her to speak French. English only was the rule. They had to hide their French books. It was a case of wanting to be proud of their heritage but also wanting to blend in.

We are so lucky to be alive at a time when we are encouraged to be proud of who we are and where we've come from. We don't have to hide anything. We can celebrate it!

We've played our music in a lot of places. We performed on TV, at the National Aboriginal Achievement Awards. And we played during the opening ceremonies at the Vancouver Winter Olympics, as part of the Indigenous Youth Gathering. That was amazing, being on such a big stage at such a huge event. And we're recording an album soon. I'm nervous about that. It's a big deal, at the best recording studio in Toronto.

Today's event is a lot smaller. We're at the Mississauga Waterfront Festival. Small events are good too because you can see the faces of the people. You can see that they are enjoying the music. One of the songs I love to play is a really fast jig from Nunavut. The elder who taught it to us said, "It's cold up there! People have to dance fast to keep warm!"

I attend a Francophone school. So many cultures come to my school, so many dialects of French, from Haiti, Somalia, Niger, all over. There are so many of us "different" ones at the school that there's no time for racism. We're all too busy just trying to get to know each other.

My brother had to deal with racism in university. You know, dumb kids making fun of him, making lame jokes. He never let it get to him. He kept playing his music and doing what he was meant to do. None of those idiots got to play at the Olympics!

The Quartet's debut album, *North West Voyage Nord Ouest*, is available through www.metisfiddlerquartet.com.

My people will sleep for one hundred years, but when they awake, it will be the artists who give them their spirit back.

— Louis Riel

Seneca, 11, and Ian, 14

The Gathering of Nations is North America's largest powwow. Three thousand dancers from more than one hundred nations all over the continent compete for prizes and honors. Held at a stadium called The Pit at the University of New Mexico in Albuquerque, the Gathering has been coming together for over thirty years. In addition to the dancing there is a music stage showcasing Indigenous talent like the hip-hop group Red Power Squad, Miracle Dolls, the Cellicion Zuni dancers, Leanne Goose and the Navajo/Osage/Apache metal band Ethnic De Generation. There are Native foods, a massive arts and crafts market and the crowning of Miss Indian World.

Seneca and Ian are two young people attending the Gathering.

Seneca

I'm a Fancy Shawl dancer and my sister, Jade, does the Jingle Dance. She's in fourth grade and her best subject is printing. I'm in fifth and reading is the thing I like most.

We've been coming to the Gathering of Nations since we were little. Our family is from the Laguna Pueblo, but we're spread out all over now. Some are in Gallup. Some are in Grants, some in Albuquerque. But we all get together at my grandmother's house in Casa Blanca on the pueblo.

I love it at the pueblo. It's not busy and crowded like the city. My grandmother has swings in her yard. We play soccer and tag — all kinds of games.

Me and my sister are Christian but we do Pueblo dancing too. Pueblo dancing is different from the dancing we're doing here at the Gathering. Fancy Shawl and Jingle dancing are more from the Plains nations. The Plains people like to share their traditional ways. That's one of the ways they keep their culture alive.

Pueblo culture is more just for us. We don't usually do it off the pueblo and there we just do it on feast and ceremony days. Pueblo clothes are different from the clothes we wear at powwows too.

Our grandmother is Cordelia Dempsey-Chee. She makes ceremonial masks out of clay. All the designs and colors have traditional meanings, but I don't know what all of them are. Our uncle is Arlan Dempsey. He makes sculptures of Pueblo dancers. Sometimes my sister and I get to help them. What I like best to do is make necklaces.

Our grandmother is a good storyteller. She tells us a lot of stories about when her great-great-grandfather was alive. Her great-great-grandfather is our great-great-great-grandfather. He lived in Tsiama village on the pueblo. Back then everyone lived like in old times, before modern things. I think I would like that, but I would miss some things too.

Grandma's father — our great-grandfather — went to the Carlisle Indian School back east. The government made him, even though he wanted to stay at home. But I think it's good that he went because he got to be there at the same time as Jim Thorpe, the famous Native runner. But he wasn't famous yet.

Grandma's family used to be sort of rich when she was a little girl. They had a ranch and they had seven kids and so much work to do they hired two African American families to help them. The men worked on the ranch and the women helped with the children. Grandma says they had so many eggs from their chickens that she and her sister used to throw eggs at each other as a game. And they had a big garden full of squash, corn and beans. Grandma said they lived by the railway tracks and lots of men would sneak onto trains because they couldn't afford a ticket, and they'd go from place to place looking for a job. My great-grandmother would give them food.

I'm not nervous anymore before dancing in a powwow. I used to be. I used to be scared that I'd do it wrong, but I'm not now. I just do my best. The judges look to see if you can keep the beat and if you are paying attention to the drum so that you stop dancing when the drumming stops.

The best part about being here is meeting kids from all over. You make a lot of new friends and celebrate your culture. And have fun!

Ian
I'm from Santo Domingo Pueblo. My family has been there for — I don't know. A long time. The pueblo used to be be-

side the Galisteo River, but the river flooded and destroyed all the homes, so the people moved to where the pueblo is now. That was over four hundred years ago, and I guess some of my ancestors go at least that far back. I don't think about it a lot. It's just where we're from.

A lot of people there still lead a very traditional life. Lots speak the language — Keresan. Children too.

It's a big place for art. Lots of people there make jewelry or pottery. It's right by an old turquoise mine, so people there have been making jewelry and things from turquoise forever. There's a big crafts market every Labor Day and people sell things from stalls along the road all the time.

August fourth is our big feast day. It's to honor St. Dominic. The pueblo is named after him, but that's the old way. The new way is to call it by its old name, which is Kewa. So we are from Kewa Pueblo.

On August fourth we have a big feast and a Corn Dance. Dancers come from other places to be a part of it. Thousands come. I'm not a dancer, but I do drumming at these special occasions and dances.

Something really bad happened there a year and a half ago. There was a big storm with lots of hail, hail the size of golf balls. It was really scary. It came down so heavy it put holes in people's cars and the roofs of their houses. Some of the homes were really old. People had lived in them for a long time, but they got flooded and destroyed, so people had to move out. And when the water dried up, it made everything moldy. You can't live in mold because it's too hard to breathe.

My dad started a foundation to help get money for the tribe to rebuild. Most people didn't have insurance. They lost everything. People were even staying in offices, just to have somewhere to stay. Dad helped do some of the actual building too.

Dad's done a lot of building in his life. He used to have a business but he lost it a couple of years ago when a fire burned up his truck and his tools. Now he and my mother make jewelry. They're good at it. They've done museum shows and other shows.

This is my first time at the Gathering of Nations. I didn't really get how big it was until I got here. There are people here from everywhere! Lots have been stopping by the booth, asking about the jewelry, just saying hello.

I don't generally see my parents during the week, so it's good to spend time with them. I go to the Santa Fe Indian School. It's a charter school, a boarding school. I'm in my second year there. I like it. The school looks good. It's not ugly. I stay in a dormitory and come home on weekends. Reading is what I like to do best. Math is sometimes a challenge.

It's a good school now because it's run by Native Americans. It used to be a boarding school run by the government. In the 1800s, kids would be taken from their families and forced to go. They'd cut the kids' hair, dress them up in military uniforms and make them march everywhere like little soldiers. And if any of them disobeyed or spoke any language that wasn't English, they got put in a jail at the back of the school and just left there.

I like being at home because we live on a ranch. We have a few horses and I like being around them.

It's a little overwhelming being here. So many people from so many places. It's really something to experience.

Nena, 16

Western science is beginning to have an apprecia-
tion for Indigenous knowledge, and there is a blend-
ing of the two approaches. NASA, for instance, has
been working with the American Indian Higher Education Consortium and other organizations. Indigenous knowledge is proving to be particularly valuable
when looking at environmental problems and decid-
ing how to correct the damage that has been done to
this planet.

In 1889, Susan La Flesche graduated from the
Women's Medical College in Pennsylvania with the
top marks in her class and became the first female
Native American physician, going on to build the first
Native American hospital. Just like Susan, Nena is
exploring the world through science. She is from the
Seminole Nation and lives in Clewiston, Florida, near
the Big Cypress Reservation.

Clewiston is a little town. We have stores like Walmart, con-
venience stores, usual things — a library, a place to get fried
frogs legs. Clewiston's nickname is America's Sweetest Town
because of the sugar refinery. Lots of times there is a sweet
smell in the air, and there are sugar cane farms all around.
When they burn the cane the air gets all smoky and it stinks.
But it's generally a nice town. Some of the whites act like
jerks, but I try to avoid them.

I go to a private school called Ahfachkee School. It's a
Seminole-run school. I like it because it reflects who I am as
a Seminole, my history and culture. And we can learn our

language. We'll do things like talk about animals using our language, and the more we learn, the more we can use it. It takes time to learn it. It's not hard. Well, yeah, it is kind of hard.

Seminoles are one of those nations that got split up during the Indian removals. A lot of our people were forced to go to Oklahoma, and there is now a Seminole Nation of Oklahoma too. But many Seminoles hid in the Everglades when the US Army came to get them, so they ended up staying. Can you imagine? You have to be tough to live in a swamp. So most of us living here now are descendants of those people.

There's Black Seminoles too. Slaves would escape and come to us — my ancestors — and we'd hide them and they became part of us. And some of the people alive today are their great-great-great-great-grandchildren.

The teachers here at this school expect us to work hard and take our work seriously. They teach us how to study, and they mix cultural practices in with our lessons, like language, basket-weaving, carving, traditional cooking, and about traditional ceremonies like the Green Corn Dance. People can visit the reservation and see displays of things like alligator wrestling, which some Seminoles in history became good at as a way to make money. Whites would pay to watch them wrestle an alligator.

I was a winner of our local science fair, which meant I got to go with a few others from our school to the National Science Fair put on by the American Indian Science and Engineering Society. My project is on color fastness — how cloth holds color. I used blueberry juice as my base and tried water with salt and other substances to see what would hold the color best. Then I did several washes with each formula, charting out what was happening.

Traditional Seminole structures, Okeechobee Seminole Reservation.

I was really excited to go to the national competition because it was in Albuquerque, New Mexico, and I'd never been anywhere before! I'd never been on a plane. I don't mind saying that I was scared, and the security stuff at the airport was so serious that it made me even more scared! But I got over it.

I loved Albuquerque. It was great, really beautiful with the mountains all around and the way they changed color as the day changed. We spent most of the time at the competition, but we still had some time to look around. We went to the science museum, went shopping at the Old Town market, we took the tramway up the mountain to see the view. And we went to the Pueblo Cultural Center, which was terrific. We learned a lot about the Pueblo people.

Before the competition we were busy. We had to check on our tables, make sure we knew which space was assigned to us, set up our projects, fix anything that had been damaged during the trip, and have everything checked over to be sure it was safe to be judged and that all the rules had been met.

Another scary thing for me was when I had to explain my project to the judges. I get really nervous when I have to talk to people I don't know. I don't often have to do it because I live and go to school where everybody knows everybody. And here were important people standing right in front of me, people who knew a lot more than me about science.

But that's why I was there. I had to explain the research methods and the conclusions. Then I got asked a lot of questions. Some I knew the answers to, some were kind of tricky, but I got through it.

Afterwards I was over-excited! I didn't know how I did so I felt really nervous about what the result would be.

Then the awards got handed out. I got a first place for chemistry!

And then I won a special award from the American Chemical Society for excellence in a project featuring chemistry!

It felt so good. The *Seminole Tribune* did a special article about us. It was really great.

But the best thing about the competition was being with so many other Native people from all over the country. All sorts of tribes — Blood, Ho-Chunk, Sauk and Fox, Kiowa, Hopi. All sorts.

Being with so many other Native kids — everywhere I looked, there were more Native kids! And we all had different backgrounds and stories, but we were all smart and into science and it was so cool.

There was an opening ceremony. People gave speeches about how proud they were of all of us, there was drumming, and one of the Native guys gave a welcoming speech in his own language, a language I hadn't heard before.

Before the national competition I was thinking about being a lawyer, but now I'm thinking I'll continue on in science. Lots of people at the science fair said I should. And there are so many areas of scientific study — botany, medicine, chemistry, lots of them.

So it was worth being nervous and scared and not giving in to it. I could have just said, No, I'm afraid to fly, I'll just stay home, and look at what I would have missed!

I'm sure there will be other things in my life that will make me afraid. But I won't let it get in the way.

José, 18

The US government referred to the Choctaw Nation as one of the Five Civilized Tribes, along with the Cherokee, Creek, Chickasaw and Seminole. They were called civilized because many had begun to adopt European ways — living in log cabins, wearing European-style clothing and attending school. But in 1829, President Andrew Jackson decided that assimilation wasn't good enough. He launched a plan to remove all Native Americans from the US South to places west of the Mississippi River. The idea was to move 60,000 Native Americans who had been living in the Eastern Woodlands since time immemorial and put them in an area vastly unsuited to their traditional way of life. The bulk of the Five Tribes were rounded up at gunpoint and then forced to walk, leaving behind farms and homes. One out of four died along the way.

Some of the Choctaw resettled in Oklahoma. Those who managed to remain behind became the Choctaw Nation of Mississippi. José is one of their descendants.

I was born in Dallas, Texas, but my parents thought it would be good for me to get away from the more negative influences of the city. So when I was twelve they sent me to the Choctaw

The robot entry from José's school.

reservation here in Mississippi to live with my grandparents. My grandparents have done so much to make me into who I am, and I'll always be grateful to my parents for sending me here.

My Dallas grandparents are retired. My grandfather made flags and my grandmother worked for the Bank of America. My mom works at Lowe's and my dad is a welder.

In Dallas, I struggled in school. I couldn't take the classes seriously. It all just seemed so unimportant. I was more interested in hanging out with friends, or with guys who weren't real friends — just other guys who liked to get into trouble. My school back in Texas had a few other Native kids, but not many. It had a mix of a lot of different kinds of kids. I knew some who were in gangs already, and others who were not yet in gangs but you could tell they were headed that way.

I didn't know about Choctaw anything really, when I

came to Mississippi. Dallas is a huge city, busy, noisy. So different from here.

I've learned a lot about my heritage since coming here. It's like my eyes were closed before. I didn't really see myself or what I could be.

I go to the Choctaw Central High School. It's big on sports and on academics. I'm in track, cross country and I used to be the captain of the soccer team. I'm president of the Beta Club and a member of Future Business Leaders of America.

My school is big on science. Our solar car team won the national title in 2010. I got involved in the Robotics Club my sophomore year. A friend told me about it. It seemed like a great fit for me. Ever since I was little, I loved playing with Legos and figuring out how things go together.

A big part of what we do is, of course, building robots, but we also do things to encourage younger kids to get excited about science. You know it can seem very serious and involved and it is, but it can also be broken down into simple concepts that younger kids can get even if they don't have any knowledge of physics. So one of the things we do is to get younger kids to build bottle rockets. They make them out of plastic soda bottles or water bottles. You add paper wings, a cylinder at the bottom, some string, this and that, put water in, pump air in it, launch it and watch it fly.

We have National Kids' Day on the reservation. All the children from the Choctaw Nation are invited to come together in one place and hang out and enjoy themselves. We do the bottle rockets with them there. I love the look on their face when they realize they can do this.

It's not building rockets that's important. Not everyone is going to be interested in rockets or robots or engineering. What's important is developing the mind, taking the gifts we've been given and building the confidence to really use them.

In the club, I am the mechanical engineer and the software engineer and I drive the robot. I construct how it will look and program it to do what it's told to. You control it with two joysticks and a laptop.

We enter competitions, competing with other schools that have robotics clubs. In two weeks we go to Duluth, Georgia, for the Peachtree Regional. That competition is called a Rebound Rumble. We all had to construct a robot that could shoot basketballs.

We see all kinds of kids at these competitions, and it's great because although we're all competing and we all want to win, we've all got science in common. So we speak a common language.

I've never been given a hard time by any of them for being Choctaw or Native American. Really, it's all about the robots at these things. But who knows? There's probably at least one kid or one adult who has preconceived ideas of what Native Americans are or can do and when our team comes in, they have to rethink all their old ideas. So that's good.

Since coming here, I've learned to speak Choctaw as well as English and Spanish. Our leaders and teachers are very big on people knowing the language. Even our sports teams, when they compete in other communities, they speak to each other in Choctaw.

My life is on a different trajectory since coming to the reservation. In Dallas the public school had so much drama. So many kids pretending to be in gangs — or maybe they really were in them! So many kids thinking the only way to feel big was to hate on somebody else. Here I don't have to worry about hate. Our tribe acts as one.

We have powwows here, but I haven't had time to really take part in them. And we have traditional games. One is called rabbit-stick hunting. Families make the rabbit sticks out of wood and throw them.

Of course I'm going to college. It was imprinted into my brain even back in Dallas that I will be a college graduate. I've applied to several schools. I want to study mechanical engineering. I hope one day to work with NASA to explore other planets.

There is great honesty in doing our best. If you don't, then you're lying to yourself.

Rachel, 15

Iqaluit is the capital and largest city of Nunavut, the vast Arctic territory stretching across Canada's North. Its population is around 7,000, two-thirds Inuit, and it's growing fast as mining increases. The city is expanding into the tundra with new housing developments to give the incoming workers places to live. It overlooks Koojesse Inlet (Frobisher Bay), which is frozen over in the winter but has massive tides in the summer.

Iqaluit's history as a community really started in 1942, with the US Air Force recruiting Inuit labor to build an airstrip. Year-round homes were built by Inuit families using building materials the airbase threw away in the local dump. The Hudson's Bay Company showed up not long after, and in 1955 Iqaluit became one of the bases of the DEW Line — an early-warning system that was supposed to let North Americans know if the Soviets were attacking with atomic weapons.

Today Iqaluit is a mixture of modern and traditional, with hide-scraping racks set up beside TV satellite dishes.

I met Rachel in her home on a hill overlooking the frozen inlet.

I'm in grade ten. I was born in Iqaluit and have lived mostly here, but I've also lived on and off in Kimmirut, which is also on Baffin Island. It takes one and a half hours to get there by small plane and six hours by Ski-Doo.

I've only done the trip once on Ski-Doo. It looked like the moon. We stopped off a couple of times in different cabins along the way. Kimmirut is small. Everyone knows everyone else.

My mother's parents are from there. My grandmother is still alive. She lived in Kimmirut until she was sixteen. She married my grandfather and came to live in Iqaluit, but they lived a nomadic lifestyle, hunting and fishing with the seasons, so really they lived in a lot of places.

She only speaks Inuk. She understands bits of English but doesn't speak it. I'm the opposite. I used to know a lot of Inuk when I was young. Now I only know how to speak a little, but I understand a lot more than I speak.

I went to an Inuk-speaking kindergarten class, but then I moved to another part of Iqaluit and the classes at that school were in English. Inuk is much more complex. English is hard too, but in Inuk, the slightest sound makes a huge difference.

There are a lot of Inuk speakers in the North — I mean, north of Iqaluit. None of my friends speak it with me unless we're joking around. We have an Inuk class at the high school, but it's an optional course. Not many kids are in it. I'm in it because I want to be a translator. I want to take a year off after high school and travel around Nunavut to the northern communities where I'll have to speak only Inuk and learn all the different styles of speaking it. That will really help me get the language deep into my brain. So I do more than the basic requirements in Inuk class because it's an opportunity to really learn something useful.

I want to be an Inuk translator for the government, maybe in the Parliament of Canada or in the Nunavut Legislature. After high school I can go on to college here and take more Inuk courses. It will be a good career but also I just want to do it to keep the language strong. I want my kids to speak it fluently, when I have kids. Language is a really important part of who we are.

English-speaking people don't understand that, because they can speak English everywhere. But if they were forced to speak only Inuk and they had no English books, they would start to feel like a part of them was lost.

I got involved with the Iqaluit Humane Society when I moved in with my foster mom, Janine. She's the local president. We have to do twenty-five volunteer hours in the community before we can graduate high school, so I initially did it just for that, but I kept on long after my required hours were done.

I clean cages, walk dogs, help out wherever I can.

It's really sad to see the neglect that some animals have to live with. Some people have a lack of value for their dogs. Others get drunk and mean and go after their dogs if the dogs get in their way.

That's not the usual thing for Inuit to mistreat their dogs. Out beyond the airport is where people keep their sled-dog teams, since they're not allowed on city streets. You can go and see for yourself that those dogs are well cared for. Inuit traditionally really depend on their dogs for hunting and for transportation. But modern life has screwed a lot of things up. Residential schools and all that's happened has made some Inuit not act in a good way. They don't have good coping mechanisms.

Poverty too. These days, some people can't afford to feed

Bilingual sign in Iqaluit.

their dogs and they call the humane society. Most dogs get shipped down to the shelter in Ottawa.

There are also a lot of dogs. Half as many dogs as there are people. There's no vet up here, so no way to spay or neuter the dogs, and if the dog is injured it can't get patched up. People shoot their injured dogs rather than watch them suffer.

There was an outbreak of canine parvovirus, which vaccinations would have prevented if there had been a vet. It makes dogs really suffer in their stomachs. When that happened, we had to clean everything with bleach — the cages, all the equipment, the walls, even the ceiling.

My birth mother is in Iqaluit. My birth father recently passed away. He was never a part of my life. I only met him once or twice. We used to talk on the telephone now and then, but not often. His other daughters — my half-sisters

Outside the high school in Iqaluit.

— said he did some work at the airport in Sanikiluaq. My mother never really talked to me about him. I never even had contact with my sisters until I was thirteen. One of them is grown now. She works for the CBC and lives here in Iqaluit. We see each other from time to time. She's great.

I've been in and out of foster homes since I was two. Things at home were harsh. Mom had a drinking problem.

I always hated going to a new home. Always. I was always scared. You walk up to a strange door and you don't know what is going to be on the other side of it. What will the foster parents be like? What will the new rules be? What will the punishments be if you break the rules? What if they already have kids and the kids don't like you?

Foster care is supposed to take you out of something unhealthy and put you in a better place. But it doesn't always work out that way.

And even if you do get put into a good foster home, it can still be hard.

There were some little girls here for a while. They'd been back and forth a few times. Their parents couldn't care for them, they'd get placed in the foster home, their parents would straighten up for a little while and get the girls back, then everything would fall apart again and the girls would come back here. There's structure here — regular things like bedtimes and meal times and baths — and they're not used to it, so they have a hard time each time they come.

I wish I had been adopted to my grandparents in Kimmirut. They adopted my second-oldest brother. I have other siblings that were adopted. My eldest sister was adopted out to my grandfather's brother. One sister stayed with her dad. My mother decided she was going to keep me, so I've been back and forth to foster care.

A lot of it goes back to what happened at the residential schools. People really got hurt there.

My grandfather was an alcoholic. My grandmother had ten children. She's raised fourteen, including me a lot of the time. She just turned seventy-eight and she's still raising my eleven-year-old cousin. He's autistic, and she still takes care of him.

This latest round of foster care for me happened because of a really bad decision I made. I made the choice to try to end my life, but really I was just wanting help. They put me into the hospital here just so that I could be safe, but there's no real treatment here. When they could get a bed for me, they sent me to a mental health treatment place in Ottawa. I was there for a while, and when I came home, I had more hope. There were therapy groups and psychologists and things to do that made me feel better.

I wish they had those things up here. There's AA up here,

but that's not enough. I was lucky. It's really hard for some people to go south for treatment.

I really love Iqaluit a lot. It's kind of like a small town, but not too small. I love the culture and how when someone needs help there's always someone around who will lend a hand. Like, there was a really bad fire recently. Lots of people turned out to help the families, donating what they could. Me and my friends talk about this a lot, about how people care about each other up here.

When I got back from treatment, they said I could either go home to live with my mother and try that again, or I could go back into foster care. I didn't think I could stay well with my mother, so I came here. I've been here for over a year. I'm doing fine.

I keep busy. I'm getting involved with Encounters with Canada. It's a program that lets you experience different things in Canada. I'm going in for sports and fitness. One of my classmates went in for medicine.

In my free time I go to the movies. The Frobisher Inn shows movies that change every three weeks. My favorite is *Law Abiding Citizen*. I'm in the school choir, in soccer, in Challenge by Choice skiing, hockey and the student council. A kamik-making class just started so I'm doing that too.

Winter is really dark most of the time and cold, but the cold is dry. If you dress for it, it's easy to manage minus 30 degrees Celsius [minus 22 Fahrenheit]. In Ottawa, minus 10 degrees feels much colder because it's so damp. In the summer there's boating and hiking. Lots of things to do.

I'd rather be Inuit today than three hundred years ago, even with all our problems. Three hundred years ago the climate was much harder. My ancestors must have had a really hard life.

I love writing fiction, mostly short stories. I even have a writer's callus on my hand! I started writing in middle school. Now I have a lot more confidence.

Today is special because it's the opening day of Toonik Tyme, our annual spring festival. It's spring even though it's minus twenty out! There are dogsled races and a huge craft sale. You have to get there early because of the line-ups. There's bannock-making contests, elders' feasts, concerts. I'm singing in the choir tonight. We're singing the Nunavut anthem. I'm going to have a great time.

Ta'Kaiya, 11

Indigenous people are often on the forefront of environmental movements because they are often the people most affected by environmental damage. When plants don't grow or game is killed off, whole ways of life can change.

Ta'Kaiya is one of the new generation of environmentalists. She is from a Coast Salish Nation and lives in Vancouver, British Columbia.

I grew up listening to my dad tell stories about times when people could go for walks and eat the mussels right off the rocks and watch whales go by and not think anything about it. They didn't have to worry about toxicity in the food, and there were so many whales, seeing one was an everyday thing.

I love hearing about traditional living on the land but I'll never be able to experience it because the world is polluted and changed. It might be that we're not too far from a time when kids like me won't be able to hear birds singing. It's so frustrating! I can't wait for corporations and governments to change and get smarter. All we have is this life and our precious Mother Earth.

My father is from the Sliammon First Nation. My mother has a British and European background. My father does social work. My mother homeschools me. I'm in grade six. My favorite things to study are the environment and ecosystems.

I'm against the Northern Gateway pipeline. They want to run a pipe all the way from the tar sands in northern Alberta through Aboriginal land in northern BC. Then they want to bring in huge supertankers to get filled up with the oil and send them out again. These supertankers are larger than the Empire State Building. The channels between all the islands are narrow. Small boats can't go through there in storms. How is a big tanker supposed to make it without having an accident?

We don't want this for our future. We don't want future generations to have to deal with this. If we don't take care of the earth there will be nothing left but mocking silence for what we could have saved.

That's why I'm standing up. We still have time to change things.

It was scary when I first starting speaking out for the environment. I didn't know people or how people would react, and I was worried I would say the wrong thing.

But then I remembered that it's the truth that I'm speaking. I shouldn't be nervous. It's something I'm passionate about. Now I'm comfortable with it.

I was part of the Freedom Train that went across the country to protest the pipeline. I loved being on the train with all the other people from other First Nations. We were all like

Northern Gateway pipeline protest rally in Toronto.

one big family and I was kind of devastated when it was over because it was such a good experience. We stopped in communities all along the way — Edmonton, Saskatoon, Winnipeg — and met people and had rallies. We finally ended up in Toronto and had a rally there too. I performed — I sing — and I spoke. Someone handed me a megaphone and I just went to it.

I sang a couple of years in a row at the annual Paddle to Swinomish. I can sing "Amazing Grace" in Sliammon, so I sang that one year, and then last year I sang a song that I wrote called "Shallow Waters." It's about the pipeline. I wrote it with Aileen de la Cruz, my music teacher. While we were working on it, there was a big oil spill in the Gulf of Mexico. So we made a CD with the song and Greenpeace sent it out to all the Members of Parliament.

I went down to Brazil, to Rio, for the UN Conference on Sustainable Development. It was a big conference for world

Ta'Kaiya speaking at the rally.

leaders on protecting the planet. I was disappointed because all these big speaking heads were not doing anything. They were not even talking about real change. They weren't really saying anything. The leaders could stand up at the conference and look all environmental without really being environmental.

But there were lots of people there who were really amazing. Lots of people doing great things, lots of Indigenous people from all around the world. They were great. Only the leaders were disappointing.

I spoke at so many public events down there. We were so busy doing so many things. We ignorantly didn't learn a few words in Portuguese before we went, so sometimes it was a little challenging!

The whole thing was pretty intense. There were lots of riots and rallies and people speaking the truth about the environment and about the conference. Once while I was speaking at a big gathering, the military came in, so I finished up quickly and got the heck out of there!

Another thing I get to do sometimes is act in films. I've been in four films. One was called *Shi-Shi-Etko*, about a girl who was sent to a residential school.

My dad was in a residential school. I used to ask him about it, and he would tell me. It hurt a lot of people. A lot of elders have some really hard stories.

There's always going to be people who frown at my family and my community. They'll be racist and think in stereotypes and say First Nations people are not smart. It's very sad that people like that are so small in their minds. But most people are not like that.

I definitely have hope about the future. We have to have hope. I guess the thing I really hope is that our leaders will smarten up in time.

We won't have tomorrow if we don't change today. We have all the answers and the solutions. We just need to make the transition from hurting the planet to helping it.

Ta'Kaiya's website is www.TaKaiyaBlaney.com.

Yinka Dene Alliance (yinkadene.ca) includes First Nations in northern British Columbia that have banned the Enbridge Northern Gateway pipelines from their territories.

Cuay, 12

Indian Nation is fast becoming Skateboard Nation, as more and more Indigenous kids take up the art and skill of skateboarding. Skateboarding is the fastest-growing sport on Native American reservations.

There is a traveling exhibit with the Smithsonian Institution called Ramp It Up — Skateboard Culture in Native America. There are Native skateboard teams such as 4-Wheel War Pony. There are also Native-owned skateboard companies like Wounded Knee Skateboards, Apache Skateboards and Full Blood Skates.

Nibwaakaawin is an organization dedicated to supporting the healthy growth of Aboriginal youth through skateboarding. They put on skateboarding clinics and camps, do school talks and are consultants to tribes who want to build skateparks on their reservations.

For the past seven years, they have been hosting the All Nations Skate Jam. Hundreds of young skaters from many tribes come together to compete in front of thousands of spectators.

That's where I met Cuay.

I'm Ojibwe from Mt. Pleasant, Michigan. My mom is from Michigan. My dad is from Kettle Point in Canada. He manages the Soaring Eagle Casino and Resort. My grampa's cousin was shot and killed by the Canadian police. His name was Dudley George. He was protesting our land being taken away so Canada shot him.

My reservation is called Saginaw Chippewa. I'm in seventh grade. My best subject is social studies. I don't always like math.

I learned to drum at school — well, I'm still learning. I started when I was six, so I've been drumming half my life. My school is on the reservation, so it's all Native American kids, which I like, because then our culture is part of every day. We don't have to put it away when the teachers want us to do something else. It's always around us.

My favorite thing to do is skateboarding. I've been doing it for three or four years. I like to go really fast. I was a little scared when I started, but now I'm used to it. The hardest trick I do — and I still haven't quite landed it — is the 540. You have to rotate on your board 540 degrees. I keep working on it. I'll get there.

We've been coming to the skate jam for years. Kids from all over are part of it. Last year we had kids from Manitoba, from Walpole Island, from Washington, all over. The pros come too, to show us things. Tony Alva's been here, and Bill Danforth — lots of pros. We come and stay all day. We eat, drum, listen to music, skate, meet everybody. It's the best.

For the competition today we're broken down into groups in our ages, and then it's beginners, intermediate and like that. I'm in the six to twelve beginners because I've only been at it a few years. We have kids here who are really good, who've been doing it for a very long time.

I'm trying to learn Ojibwe. Our community has only a few elders left who speak it. It's hard. I only know a little bit. I dance too. I do the Fancy War Dance.

Cuay skateboarding.

When I do these things, I think about who I am and all the people who did the drumming and the dancing before me.

I'm more Ojibwe than American. The white Americans have wanted to get rid of us for hundreds of years, but we're still here. There used to be a saying, "Kill the Indian to save the man." Which means to get rid of the Indian part, which they thought was bad. Really what the saying means is, "Kill the Indian to save the white man." But, like I said, we're still here!

Jeffrey, 18

In 1949 the Hoover Commission outlined a policy of termination, through which it sought to force Native Americans into white society by simply declaring that their tribes no longer existed. The motive was to get Indigenous people off land that mining and energy companies wanted to exploit. From 1953 to 1962, termination was the official policy of the US government — 109 tribes were told they didn't exist anymore, including the Klamath in Oregon and the Menominee from the Wisconsin area. More than one million acres of Native land was taken from them, and more than 13,000 Native Americans lost all tribal affiliation.

Indigenous peoples have a history of fighting for their rights, in groups such as the All Indian Pueblo Council — which formed initially in 1598 and then was renewed in the 1920s — and the National Congress of American Indians, which began in 1944. The termination policy galvanized a new era of activism, and the National Indian Youth Council was formed in 1961.

United National Indian Tribal Youth (UNITY) is an organization that brings together Native young people and trains them to be leaders in their local communities and on national issues. It started thirty-five years ago and now has 150 youth councils all over the

United States and Canada. Every summer there is a conference with speakers, workshops and renewing of spirit.

I met Jeffrey at the UNITY conference in Minneapolis.

I come from the Watuppa Wampanoag Reservation on Martha's Vineyard, an island off the coast of Massachusetts. Wampanoag means People of the First Light. We're the first to see the sun in the morning. It was my ancestors who greeted the Pilgrims when they landed on Plymouth Rock, and my ancestors helped them survive through the first winter. When you think of Thanksgiving, think of us.

There were thousands of us before the Europeans came. The invaders brought epidemics, and they captured lots of us and turned us into slaves and shipped us to the Caribbean. There's a Wampanoag community in Bermuda today that comes from the slave trade hundreds of years ago.

Now Martha's Vineyard is like a playground for rich and famous people. President Bill Clinton went there for a holiday. So did the Obamas, Reese Witherspoon, all kinds of writers and celebrities. They sail and go shopping and eat in the restaurants.

I've lived on the reservation all my life. My mother is from there. I don't know my biological dad. My stepfather moved in with us when I was six. He works at the post office. My mother just had another baby, so I have a new brother.

On the island the rez is thirty minutes from everything. It's hard for people to move around unless they have a car, so it can seem very isolated.

There's one high school on the island and there was a lot of racism there. You get squashed for being Native. And for not having money. Like I said, some of the families on the island are rich. Not all of them. After all, someone has to do the work for the rich people!

Some of the white adults would be on your side, but a lot of them would cheat you. Like at basketball, the coach would give more playing time to the rich white kids, even if the Indian kids were better players. I'd look down the bench and see all these brown faces. We all knew what was happening.

The rich kids got stuff handed to them. They had nice clothes, but they didn't take care of them. They had expensive cars, all the latest toys. They didn't care.

We had to fight for everything we got.

When I was growing up, I had no real idea what it meant to be Indian. It did not seem like anything special. It felt like a disadvantage.

One of my friends started up a youth council on the reservation a few years ago. I didn't get involved at first because I didn't think it would go anywhere. But she kept on at me to work with her, and because I liked her, I gave it a try. It made me feel a little stronger, a little more hopeful.

And then I went to a UNITY conference in Oklahoma, and my whole world changed. I couldn't believe there were all these young Indians who were proud to be Indian, who knew about their culture, who were strong and spoke up for themselves, sometimes in their original languages!

At this year's conference we have over 1,500 youth from many different tribes and communities. They've come here to plan, to meet others, and to get energized so they can go back to their home communities feeling strong and ready to work.

The experience of that first conference transformed me. Seeing so many tribal youth proud to be who they are! So many tribal adults cheering them on, encouraging them, ex-

Procession at the UNITY conference in Minneapolis.

pecting them to be strong and do well, telling them that what they do is important, that the decisions they make can lift up their entire nation.

After I came back from Oklahoma full of stories, my mother was inspired to get more involved in the community too. I was so encouraged! I wanted to carry that feeling with me all the time. She now works as an advisor to the local youth council.

Before I got involved I felt empty, angry and alone. I believed all the negative messages. I couldn't imagine any sort of future for myself. Just more emptiness.

If UNITY hadn't come into my life, I don't even want to think about what my life would be like. I get chills just thinking about it, with some of the stuff I was into. I certainly wouldn't be where I am or what I am today. It's the people of UNITY who tell you to believe in yourself. It's the love, the encouragement. It's the way your life is touched and the way you learn to touch the lives of others. It's also the high expectations that are put on you. You are expected to do well, to challenge yourself and be a good example. It's because of the stakes being so high. The weight of history is on you, but there are lots of people around to help you carry that weight. And if you slip, they are there for you and they get you back on track.

Where I come from, when you leave the rez, no one cares about you. You might as well be invisible.

I went back to my reservation all energized and got really involved with my youth council. I got elected vice president and started learning all I could from older kids and anyone who would teach me. Learning about my culture and history and how to work with others. After two years of being vice president, I got elected president.

I also became a representative from my council to the UNITY conference. Once you become a rep, you get to go to the leadership trainings and meet reps from all over Indian country. You really get to see the work that goes into building an organization. You learn how to learn, how to facilitate others learning and doing. I bring new things back to my community after every meeting.

The conference is busy all the time, every day. There are workshops and meetings, guest speakers and music. On one night there is a cultural show. Youth show off the dances and regalia of their tribe or nation. Another night there's a talent show. All kinds of kids showing all kinds of talent.

The welcome was given by Bea Shawanda, an elder from Manitoulin Island. She told us that UNITY means standing together and keeping distractions at bay, so that we can learn what's really important, that our traditions and culture provide answers for everything. Our mothers and fathers and grandparents and ancestors fought and died so that we could be here.

Grandpa Sky, the elder who started the first UNITY Fire, is here with us too. The fire is the sacred fire that burns through the whole conference. It is set up in the parking lot of this hotel. There's a canopy to keep the elders out of the hot sun and the rain. Anyone can go and sit by the fire and talk or just be. Grandpa Sky was honored today. He is in a wheelchair and he came to the front of the auditorium and a special blanket was put around his shoulders. He told us that what you do from your mind and heart is worth more than any dollar bill that there is. After he spoke, kids lined up to greet him — a long, long line of kids who just wanted to have a moment with this good man.

Native youth are hungry to be connected to something. They can find that connection here and in the traditions of their own communities. Sometimes they have to go looking for it, but as long as they believe it's out there, they'll find it.

We have elders at our conference who were part of the early days of putting UNITY together. I look at them, then I look at the fifteen-year-olds who are here for the first time. I can see that these young kids are going to become strong, powerful leaders for the Indian Nation. It makes me really proud.

Our leaders don't take it easy on us just because we're young. One of the adult leaders on the first day said, "Your grandparents think you're cute. Well, you aren't cute to me. You are leaders. You need to be serious and know that you can make a difference now. You don't have to wait ten or twenty or thirty years. In fact, you can't wait that long. There are kids your age who commit suicide, who have given up on themselves or are strung out on drugs and alcohol. They can't wait any longer for help, and you can't wait any longer to step up."

He said, "You are the ones who have to embrace Indian youth, that if the youth are lost, then all of us, our history, our culture, our ancestors, all are lost. You are the loss of us or the return of us."

It's a big responsibility, but it's no bigger than what our ancestors did for us. And what we do, we do for the Native youth who will follow us, seven generations from now.

It's on us now.

I shall see our young braves and our chiefs sitting in the houses of law and government, ruling and being ruled by the knowledge and freedom of our great land. So shall we shatter the barriers of our isolation. So shall the next hundred years be the greatest in the proud history of our tribes and nations.

— Chief Dan George, Tsleil-Waututh First Nation (Burrard Band of North Vancouver)

Marissa, 14

The Cherokee Nation's original homeland is in the eastern United States, in the area around North Carolina and Tennessee. When gold was discovered on this land, the Cherokee were forced by the government on a long walk out of their territory. This became known as the Trail of Tears, as many lives were lost along the way.

The Cherokee Nation settled in Oklahoma. Marissa has been singing with the Cherokee National Youth Choir for three years.

I've been all over the United States with the choir, from California on the west coast to North Carolina on the east coast. I've been all over Oklahoma. We sing in the smallest churches in the smallest towns and the biggest amphitheaters, for Native audiences and for mixed audiences. We go into a lot of Native American churches to sing, and we perform at festivals and conferences. It's fantastic. I get to go to a lot of cool places and meet interesting people from all over the world. We've met some famous people too. When the Tulsa Hard Rock opened up — it's owned by the Cherokee — our principal chief wanted our choir to be the first performers on the stage. We sang "The Star-Spangled Banner" and a blessing song. We opened for the group Foghat.

My grandmother works for the Cherokee Nation archives and she told me about the choir because she knows I love to sing. I had to audition for a place. The audition was scary because I had to sing in front of people I'd never met before.

But I'm glad I didn't let the fear stop me because joining the choir is the best thing I've ever done.

The audition was really the easy part. Once you join the choir, the hard work starts. You have to learn the Cherokee language. All our songs are in Cherokee, except for "The Star-Spangled Banner." We sing the first half of that in Cherokee and the second half we sing in English.

Cherokee is hard! It's completely different grammar from English. Instead of letters it uses syllabary — 86 different characters that relate to the sounds or syllables in the words. Once you catch on, it's easy. Well, maybe not easy, but once you train yourself to learn the syllabary and think a different way about words, then you can get it. I like knowing it.

When we perform, we wear traditional Cherokee clothing. Girls wear traditional dresses made with cotton and ribbon. Guys wear ribbon shirts — cotton shirts with ribbon sewn on them vertically and horizontally.

We also wear a lot of Native American jewelry, but not a lot of the turquoise that most people think of as Native jewelry. Turquoise isn't from Cherokee territory. We make clay bead necklaces. We roll bits of clay into little beads and run a string through them. We make corn bead necklaces too.

The Cherokee people now living in Oklahoma are the descendants of those who ended up here after the Trail of Tears

The Cherokee of Oklahoma don't have a reservation. We have our tribal headquarters in Tahlequah and we have legislative jurisdiction over fourteen counties.

I find it interesting to think of how what happened in history decides what's going on today. I live in Oklahoma instead of North Carolina because of what people decided back in the 1800s. So I have to think about my decisions carefully, to be careful to have a good result in the future.

My mother works as the housing manager at the university, helping students find a place to live. My father is an LPN at the hospital.

When I look around at the other members of the choir, I sometimes think about all the people we're related to in the past, that all our families had roles to play in the history of the Cherokee people. My friend Sophie, one of her relatives was Hair Conrad. He was a Cherokee council member at the time of the Trail of Tears.

But I don't think about that too much, especially not during rehearsals because we're kept busy working then.

These days we're starting work on a CD of patriotic songs. Right now we're learning the songs. In the summer we'll go to a recording studio in Tulsa to record them.

The choir has many CDs out now. I've been involved with a few of them. Being in a recording studio is awesome! There's a kitchen with drinks and snacks and most of the time the studio people will say you can have anything you want out of the fridge! And there are lots of places to lounge and relax while other people are recording. We don't goof around though. Being there out in the professional world makes us want to act like professionals. But it is really cool to say, "I've just spent the day in the recording studio!"

When a lot of people think of Native Americans they think about poverty and drug abuse and bad schools. I know there are communities that struggle with that. I've heard about the residential schools and Native Americans being stuck on reservations where the soil is rocky and won't grow anything. It's terrible, and people should know about it so it can get better.

But people should also know that in the Cherokee district, we have great schools. The high school uses a lot of technology. Every student has their own laptop. We have opportunities to go everywhere and do everything. I think Indian country has some of the worst schools in the United States and it also has some of the best.

The future is wide open to me.

The Cherokee National Youth Choir is on Facebook.

We know our lands are now become more valuable: the white people think we do not know their value; but we are sensible that the land is everlasting, and the few goods we receive for it are soon worn out and gone.

> — Canassatego-Mingo,
> Six Nations Chief

Lane, 14

Lacrosse originated with the people of the Ongwe- honwe Haudenosaunee, or Six Nations, the People of the Longhouse — Tuscarora, Mohawk, Oneida, Seneca, Cayuga and Onondaga. Sim- ilar games were played by other nations like the Semi- nole, Choctaw and Sioux. Also known as the Ancient Game or the Creator's Game, its purpose was — and for some still is — spiritual. It is offered up to the Cre- ator as a prayer for healing or as an expression of gratitude. Some people are given miniature lacrosse sticks when they are born, and when they pass on to the next life, a lacrosse stick is placed next to them in the casket.

Lane is in grade nine. He is part of the latest gen- eration of lacrosse players in his family.

I'm from the Iroquois Confederacy, and I live on the Six Na- tions Reserve on the Grand River in southern Ontario. I have four brothers and four sisters. I'm in the middle. My father works in security and my mother passed away when I was young. I live on the reserve with my dad's mom, her daughter and boyfriend and their baby and one sister and little cousins.

I've been playing lacrosse for over ten years. When I was really small, my dad put a little lacrosse stick in my hand, and that was that. It's like I was born to it. And I sort of was.

There are at least six generations of lacrosse players in my family. My family has been on this land for at least six generations. Probably a whole lot longer than that.

My grandfather is still alive. He used to play on a lacrosse team and he got paid for it too. He also worked in factories.

I play on three teams — the Six Nations Warriors Home Club, Team Iroquois, which is a Canadian national team, and Edge Lacrosse. Edge does mostly exhibition games, the sort of games scouts come to looking for players to give scholarships to. It's Native and non-Native, but the white kids on the team don't give us any hassles. They love the game as much as we do.

I'm hoping to go to Syracuse University on a lacrosse scholarship. I'd want to study something in the field of science. Environmental science, maybe, or biology, or maybe space science. Not sure yet.

My home is only five minutes away from this arena, so I'm here usually at least four days a week. I love it. They know me here and they give me responsibilities. I like helping out and being a part of things.

One of the things I do is help out with girls' teams. I play in goal for the Six Nations Under 15 Girls. They don't have a goalie.

Lacrosse has been played by my people since forever, since long before your people came here. The Iroquois played it, the Lakota, the Seminole, the Choctaw. We all played some version of it.

Winning or losing isn't the point. We play it to honor the Creator who made us. So we have to play the very best we can, all the time.

Lacrosse was also traditionally a way of working out disagreements between tribes. It's also used as a healing ceremony, a form of medicine, and to get warriors ready and in shape for war.

Lacrosse is a fast game. When we play in the arena, there are eighteen runners and two goalies. When we play in a field outside, there can be forty players.

We didn't name it lacrosse. The French priests called it that back in the 1600s. They said that the stick reminded them of the Shepherd's Cross, which in French is la crosse.

My ancestors used a game of lacrosse to attack a British fort. It was in the 1700s, I think. The British kicked out the French but were not treating the Native people very well. So the Natives made a plan. They started a big lacrosse game outside the fort. The British soldiers all watched and got drunk and forgot about doing their jobs. One of our warriors tossed a ball inside the fort, and the drunk British soldiers just opened the door and let them walk in to get it. And that's when the warriors attacked!

I love being at the lacrosse arena. You walk in and it's clean and bright with shiny white walls. There are photos of Gaylord Powless and Bill Isaacs, probably two of the greatest players who ever lived. They came from here. They have old team jerseys in a display case, team photos from really long ago in the 1960s. You know you're a part of something that has gone way back, and this is just the present day of it. It will go way into the future too.

When I play at big games and there's lots of cheering, I think of it being the same cheering that happened hundreds of years ago, and I feel like I'm someone who lived and played a long time ago or that someone who lived and played a long time ago is living again when I play. It's hard to explain.

When I'm not here at the arena I hang out with my cousins. I go to traditional things on the reserve. Powwows and

Aboriginal Day and things like that. Every year we have Bread and Cheese Day, to remember when Queen Victoria said she would give us bread and cheese to thank us for our help in the War of 1812. Well, she started off giving us blankets, but switched to bread and cheese because that was a lot cheaper. It's a big day with music and rides at the fair grounds. I like techno music and traditional music, and my favorite food is corn soup. I don't have a pet personally, but my aunt who I live with has a hairless cat named Varekai. She bought it online.

When I go to Brantford to shop at one of the malls, sometimes I hear people — white people, adults and kids — saying racist things, and I think, oh, grow up, and then I get on with my day.

Cassie, 17

Cassie attends Frontier Collegiate in Cranberry Portage. It's a boarding high school in northern Manitoba for students from remote fly-in communities that have no high school of their own. It used to be a military base, and remnants of the base can still be seen around the school. Although there have been great strides forward in online education, barriers still exist, such as access to computers and over-crowded, poorly constructed homes that make studying impossible. Students who attend Frontier must choose between being with their families and being educated.

Cassie's family lives in Cormorant, a small community in Manitoba.

I was born in The Pas, but lived in Cormorant my whole life. Cormorant is small and you know everybody. If you don't know what to do with yourself, you just walk outside and meet someone you know and maybe they'll suggest something.

In the summer there's swimming at the bridge. The town is on a lake by a provincial park so it's pretty. There's camping at Moose Lake and hunting. That's what my family usually does for Thanksgiving and Easter. I went moose hunting once when I was younger. It was scary because I was quite young and there was a lot I didn't know about surviving and being in the wild. Plus I'd heard the stories about how bad-tempered moose can get.

I go chicken hunting on my own. I take my dog and off we go. It's exciting to see something moving around in the bush and you know you can turn it into a good meal for your family. And I love bass fishing. I just catch them and my brother or Dad or Papa or Grandma clean them.

My mother was born in Cormorant and my dad was born in Nelson House, Manitoba. He's part of the Nisichawaya-sihk Cree First Nation.

His father was taken to a residential school, Red Deer Industrial School. It was really bad there. He was really traumatized.

He managed to run away from the school when he was sixteen. He made it home to see his mother but she had died eight years before. The school didn't bother to tell him.

While he was back home he met my grandmother and they had my dad. They were so afraid Dad would be taken away. The government would just swoop in and take kids. They took him and a couple of the older girls in the community who were also at risk of being taken by the government and they hid them away on the trapline. They just stayed in the bush all year round. My grandfather would see them when he could. He worked some distance away and could only get the train when his work would let him.

My father was eighteen or nineteen when he came off the trapline. Since then, all he's done is work. He said he felt dumb because he couldn't read, but he still got a lot of work on building sites because he was so strong and capable. He helped build the Super 8 Motel in The Pas.

He knows how to read a little now. He learned along with

Gathering circle at Cassie's school.

me when I was going to school, but he's very slow at it. I do most of his reading for him.

I love my dad and I'm really proud of him.

His father was an alcoholic from being traumatized at the residential school. Dad started drinking when I was young, so Mom kicked him out. She didn't want us to be around that kind of chaos. I only got to really know him when I was twelve or thirteen.

He fought forest fires in British Columbia for a while. At one fire a tree fell and hit him, sent him rolling off down a hill. He was hurt bad in that. Two years after that he was driving down the highway and a semi truck slid on a patch of ice and slammed into his car. His legs were smashed so bad that a lot of his bone had to be replaced with metal.

He's doing pretty good now. He's quit drinking. He's on pain pills which he wants to get off of, but every time he tries to quit he says it feels like there are bugs crawling all over him and he gets really sick. Those pain pills are terrible things.

Mom graduated from high school. She's a counselor now at the school.

Cormorant is mostly Métis. Some families have been there for generations. One of the girls I know at this school, her ancestor was one of the founders of the town, and her family is still there.

A lot of the houses are crowded and in bad shape, and people have to wait a really long time for a new house. Most have way more people living in them than they have room for. They sleep in living rooms, on kitchen floors, wherever. It's that way for a lot of kids in a lot of communities. When they come to this school they get their own room in the dorm and they're not used to it, so they'll double up, sleep on their neighbor's floor, just because they feel too alone at night.

Cormorant is nice. It's quiet and surrounded by bush. A lot of the houses are run-down though. It looks like people are really just hanging in. But there's stuff to do like walk on trails through the bush. People set traplines just like their ancestors did. We have Métis Days, Aboriginal Days. In the winter there's snowshoeing, goose and moose calling. It's good. I like it. But it's hard too, living there. When something bad happens, it's really hard to get away.

I like this school. I like the computer lab, the library, and that there are traditional singers and drummers. There's not much to do in the town. Most of the shops are shut. There's a little store we all walk to where we can get chips and chocolate bars and burgers, but there's no place to sit and eat your burger. You have to take it with you.

I'm good at my classes, like math, English, biology. All of them, really. I'm not yet sure what I want to do. I think I'd like to adopt a kid when I get older. My mother does respite care for the Children's Aid. She watches kids and takes them to see their parents. I think I would like to adopt because then I can have a child without having to deal with the child's father. A husband would be more work than a kid. It would be easier to do it all myself.

When I was fourteen, I couldn't stand Cormorant anymore and needed to get out. I moved in with Dad. He was living in The Pas, and then we moved to Winnipeg. The city seemed like a lot of work. I had to take a long bus ride to get to school. I couldn't just walk down the path. And there were all these cars and all these people and so much noise. I didn't like it. I wasn't ready for it.

I'm graduating from high school this year and then I'm off to college.

I'm ready for the city now.

Western movies always seemed to show Indian women washing clothes at the creek and men with a tomahawk or spear in their hands, adorned with lots of feathers. That image has stayed in some people's minds. Many think we're either visionaries, "noble savages," squaw drudges or tragic alcoholics. We're very rarely depicted as real people who have greater tenacity in terms of trying to hang on to our culture and values system than most people.

— Wilma Mankiller, first female chief of the Cherokee Nation

Justyce, 9

Fort Berthold, North Dakota, is land belonging to the Three Affiliated Tribes. In 1837, three-quarters of the people there were wiped out by smallpox brought in by settlers in the footsteps of Lewis and Clark.

Traditionally a farming people, their good farmland was flooded out when the Garrison Dam was built in the 1950s to control flooding elsewhere along the Missouri River. It is said that some stayed on their land to meet the rising water. Although the community fought long and hard to try to stop the dam, whole villages were buried under what is now Lake Saka-kawea, including the Fort Stevenson Indian School, a harsh place where students who tried to run away were locked up in the guardhouse.

In payment for the farmland being flooded, the fed-eral government promised commodity foods — gener-ally canned, processed foods very different from the traditional diet of the Three Affiliated Tribes. High rates of type 2 diabetes on the reservation can be traced back to that dam.

In more recent years, it's been discovered that Fort Berthold sits on top of the Bakken oil field. Fifty-seven oil wells now dot the reservation, and trucks rumble through formerly silent valleys twenty-four hours a day. A huge influx of unaccompanied male workers from outside the community has led to an increase in crime, a drastic rise in food prices, a massive housing shortage, brothels being set up in motels and a growing illegal drug problem.

At least seven children have been killed by the oil trucks. The increase in traffic has also killed a lot of deer, making the traditional deer hunt — one of the ways people have of getting quality food — very difficult.

One of the havens for children is the Boys and Girls Club. There are six of these clubs on the Fort Berthold Reservation. Justyce and her sister, Journey (shown on the left in the photo), go to the club in New Town, created after the building of the dam. The club meets in the town's community center, right beside an oil well. The staff do daily checks of carbon monoxide levels and have an evacuation plan in place should the well explode or leak — something that has already happened in another part of the reservation.

We live in New Town now but our parents are from White Shield. Our mom is a nurse and our dad works in oil. Our stepdad works in construction and our stepmother works at home.

We've been coming to the Boys and Girls Club since we

were little. We do all sorts of things — basketball, field trips, art. I love tissue paper art. You know, when you wind tissue paper around pencils and make art out of it.

My sister loves to fix hair. Mom got her a model doll's head with real hair and she practices doing hairstyles on it. Mom taught her how to do a French braid. She wants to be a hair stylist when she gets older. I want to open up a spa where you can get a massage and get your nails done.

We belong to the Three Affiliated Tribes — the Arikara, the Hidatsa and the Mandan. By the casino where we go swimming with the Boys and Girls Club there's a museum that will tell you all about it. They have things there like old baskets and rattles and ceremonial clothes and old weapons.

We do so much with the Boys and Girls Club. In the summer there's a culture camp at Earth Lodge Village by New Town on the reservation. We go to the earth lodges, these round buildings like where our ancestors used to live. We have Amazing Races up the hills. We have an activity room at the center where we can play Twister or chess or do homework. They take us horseback riding, to play golf and sometimes we go bowling. Sometimes we just flop down on the cushy red sofa and read or talk.

There's a list of rules on the wall, like Be nice, Ask before leaving the room, Clean up after yourself, No bullying. And there's a big fish tank in there too.

Journey and I also dance at powwows and at Zumba. Journey dances traditional and I dance Fancy Shawl.

It's been scary here since all the oil workers started coming. It used to be just us. It was really quiet, no cars on the road. But now it's noisy all the time.

All these strange men are here now. They live in big Man Camps full of trailers and in motels, all these white men. We

Traditional roundhouse, Fort Berthold Reservation.

don't know who they are. They drink and they fight. It makes us scared to be outside.

I'm scared of them. Some of them like to steal little kids. One time Journey and her friend were headed down the street. I was following along behind them. I was looking at my hand because I had a cut on my hand. I sort of saw this guy sitting and watching us, and when I passed him he reached out and tried to grab at me. I ran away. We all ran home. Another time my grandpa came and banged on our door. He told us to stay inside, that there was some guy going around looking for kids.

I don't know if that guy was caught or if he just went away.

Big trucks come through here all the time now, really big ones. And all the highways are torn up to make them bigger so they can bring in even more trucks. The trucks go really fast. So fast that little kids can't always get out of the way. A bunch of kids have been killed that way.

Our brother was killed because of one of those trucks.

His name was Jordy and he loved to play basketball and frisbee. He had a frisbee that lighted up when it got dark out. He was twenty-one.

He was a really good brother, not mean or anything. Everybody liked him. He used to have a dog that died, named Kimber. He was so sad when Kimber died that he kept Kimber's collar on his keychain.

He died on March 4, just a few months ago. I remember because I was at my friend's birthday party and someone came to pick me up and tell me what happened. Now I'll never be able to go to my friend's birthday party again because Jordy's memorial will always be on the same day.

We will probably stay here because our brother is buried here. You have to love the place where your family is buried. We won't want to leave because then Jordy will be alone.

Tyrone, 13

Rossbrook House in Winnipeg, Manitoba, was started in 1976 as a safe drop-in center for kids in the inner city. It is open every day from eight in the morning until midnight and twenty-four hours a day during school holidays and weekends. Five thousand people a year use its services. In addition to the drop-in center, where there is food, clothing, counseling and recreation, Rossbrook House runs schools for First Nations and Métis kids not able to make it in the mixed public system. Eagles' Circle is a school for older kids.

I met Tyrone at Eagles' Circle.

My parents come from Berens River, Manitoba. You can only get there by flying in most of the year. In the winter there's an ice road that goes down to Bloodvein First Nation.

Kids at this school belong to a lot of different reserves — Ebb and Flow, Hollow Water, Pine Creek, God's Lake. They're Ojibwe, Cree, Dene.

The good thing about Winnipeg is that the hospitals are close by. There's lots of recreation, lots of houses and lots of friends and family.

The hard thing is that there are a lot of gangs — Native gangs, white gangs, black gangs. There's violence, lots of drugs. I've seen both things — people doing drugs and selling drugs, and people beating each other up. It's hard not to see it. A friend of mine was jacked for his bike. He'd saved up for it and just bought it. It cost $130. A group of white kids came up to him. They had a can of bear mace. They sprayed it in his face and took his bike.

It stings. Lots of kids I know have had people spray them with it. Another kid here knows of a gang that attacks people with machetes. There are a lot of different gangs.

The north end of Winnipeg is the baddest place. My friend Ronald — he's an Ojibwe from the Ebb and Flow reserve — he lives in the safer part of the north end. Well, it's supposed to be safer, but some white guy pulled a knife on him and told him to hand over his backpack. But he swung the pack at the guy instead, knocked him off his bike and got away.

In my house I have one brother, one sister, nephew, niece, Mom and me.

My other brother, Ramsay, is in jail. He's twenty-four. They're saying he did second-degree murder at a bus stop over in Portage. He's been in jail for three months. My mother goes to visit him and says it's really hard to see him there. I haven't gone yet. I miss him, but Mom says he told her he doesn't want me to see him cry. He doesn't want to see me cry either.

Maybe I could write to him. I don't know what I'd say, but I want him to know I haven't forgotten him. He's a really good brother. He loves to cook. He'll make these great meals for us, then we eat together and it's really fun. He plays games with me too. He doesn't ignore me because I'm younger.

My dad passed away when I was eight. He drank a lot. He was a good dad though. He bought us candy and a computer game, but it wasn't good to see him drinking. It was hard to know how to be around him because you never knew what would make him angry.

Sometimes he'd come by and you could tell he'd been drinking so Mom didn't want him in the house. She wouldn't answer the door. He'd be banging on it and calling to us but she wouldn't let him in. She said we needed to be safe more than he needed to see us.

My sister is fourteen. She's sort of bossy. She's in high school now. She's smart. And she's strong like my mother.

My oldest sister lives somewhere else with her boyfriend. She just had a new baby. Her other children live with us. My nephew is only four and he can already use a computer. He learned when he was only three! He was born with teeth. I wonder if that means he's special or smart in some way.

Berens River — Pukatawagan — I've been up there with my mom. She wanted to go back and I wanted to see it. It's quiet up there and beautiful, but there's lots of violence.

Before I was born, there were people driving around in their boats one night. They had rifles and were shooting at houses. Mom said everyone turned their lights out so the shooters couldn't find anything to shoot at. She doesn't know why they were shooting or who they were. She thinks they were probably drunk. They may have been from the reserve. They might also have been white men who go there to hunt and fish. They've bothered our people before. You have to stay away from them because they think it's far away from everything and they can just do what they want.

Violence has happened at my house here too. My brother Ramsay got into some stuff with a gang, and then these guys — not his friends, some other guys — broke our window and pointed guns at us. They were mad about something.

When my nephew was only one year old, my sister was

sitting with him in her lap. Someone threw a rock through the window, then sprayed mace inside. Some of it got my little nephew. I think it was also done by people who were angry at my brother. If you get in with a gang and you don't do exactly what they say, they get mad at you and do these terrible things to your family.

Ramsay calls us from jail sometimes. He says that he misses everybody. He asks me about school. He says I should study hard and stay away from gangs.

We're still in the same neighborhood, in the same house. It's been quiet there since my brother was arrested.

My mother works for CFS — Child and Family Services — helping kids get into foster homes and group homes. She's a social worker.

We once took in a foster kid named Sammy. He was with us for a year, a Native kid. A great guy, older than me. I liked him a lot. He's in jail now.

I go to sweat lodges out of town. They help me get cleansed. I'm tired when I come out of a sweat, like I've been away on a long trip. Seven to nineteen rocks are put into a fire to get hot. A sweat is about being in a big circle. It's like Mother Earth's womb. When you go in, you are going back — back in time, back to your culture, back to the core of what's important, back to the Creator, back to the earth. When you come out you feel warm and happy.

I go to a Sun Dance too. It's held near Selkirk. They have this circle. On the first day you feast and dance. On the second day you do a fruit and vegetable feast, that's all, and you dance. You're woken up at seven, go to the sweat lodge, rest, then start dancing at nine. Boys put a cloth around their waist. Girls wear dresses. This goes on for four days. The third day is a fast. Kids can exit out of the circle at any time and go to a tepee and eat. After we dance, we rest.

On the fourth day, we dance until noon. Then we take the circle apart and take down the tree of life and take down our tents. Then we eat.

It makes me feel good because this year I actually completed it. On the second day it was really hard. The weather was hot and I felt like quitting. But I found the strength to keep going and I completed it.

I like being who I am and being from where I'm from. It's special.

My advice to other Native kids is to keep on going to cultural things. Even if you don't see the point right away. The culture will keep you clean and safe. It will give you something to do that's important, with people who really want you to do well. Not like gangs, who only want to use you.

Brittany, 17

The use of Indigenous names and caricatures in sports teams is an on-going issue. Some sports fans are adamant about their right to do the "tom-ahawk chop" and wear feathered headdresses to games. When Native Americans protested the name Cleveland Indians and the baseball team's logo, Chief Wahoo, they were met by folks who spat on them and pelted them with beer cans.

The Washington Redskins football team has been sued to get it to change its name. "Redskin" was first used to refer to the bloodied scalps of Native Americans taken by white men to be exchanged for bounty payment. The 1755 Phips Proclamation gave permission to the settlers to kill all the Penobscot Indians. It laid out how much money the government would pay for each dead Indian — fifty pounds sterling for adult male scalps, twenty pounds for each child.

People are becoming aware of how insulting these names and caricatures are to Indigenous people, and are starting to change things. Boards of education in Oregon, Wisconsin, Maine and other states have voted to ban Native American mascots in state schools.

Brittany is a young athlete from Ontario who has

I started running when I was in grade six. It was fun. It's easy to do. How I do in a race depends only on me, not on what the rest of the team does. It's gotten more intense as I've gotten into higher levels of competition, but it's still fun.

Running has taken me all over. Lots of in-Canada meets, of course, and I went to Italy in 2009 to the IAAF World Youth Championships in Bressanone.

My best events are the 400 meters and the 400-meter hurdles. I got eleventh overall, and third place out of the other sixteen-year-olds. That means I was the third-fastest sixteen-year-old on the planet!

There were young people there from all over the world — Kenya, Australia, everywhere. They allowed kids to compete in the way they felt most comfortable. Some ran all seven laps in their bare feet! Seven laps on hard track!

It was my first time flying. My mom and grandma joined me there a couple of days after I went. I had to go early to get over jet lag and get used to the higher altitude. Bressanone is in the mountains. It was a bit of a challenge for me. I have a touch of asthma and had to use my puffer. It rained a lot too — thunder, lightning, everything.

No one talked English in this little town except for us foreigners from English-speaking places. It was great being surrounded by so many different languages.

All the Canadians stayed at the same hotel so that we could feel more like a team.

We all had to pay our own way to Italy, and my family doesn't have a lot of spare money. So the community took it on. There was a powwow on the reserve. First the chief made a speech honoring me and the other youth of the community. Then the Blanket Dance started. People danced and threw money on the blanket, and that's how I was able to go to Italy with my family.

The community didn't just give me money. They also followed me on the internet and Facebook so I really felt backed up by everyone when I was on the other side of the world. It was like they were all over there with me.

When the Olympic torch relay came through this area, the community chose me to carry the torch through the reserve. It was so exciting! Everyone was lined up along the street, cheering and waving. I felt so tall and proud running through all that.

I haven't had to deal with too much racism, probably because my skin is fairly pale and I could pass for white. Other students from my reserve have had a lot of stupid stuff thrown at them by white kids and adults. Because some people take me for white, white people will say racist things to me about other Natives. I usually challenge it. Sometimes I don't have the energy.

Even white people who know I'm Native can sometimes act like jerks. They'll say, "Heading home to your tepee?" or go "Woo woo woo woo!" and pound their hands on their lips, doing some lame Hollywood version of a war dance.

Others ask me questions, and some of the questions are fine. You can tell when people really want to know something in order to get to know you better. But some questions go too far. Like, because I'm Ojibwe they think I was born on some sort of different spiritual plane or something. All these white people who want to be Native because "Native culture is so beautiful." It's another way of not seeing me as human. It's another way of being racist.

A lot of First Nations kids struggle. They don't think they

can make it. They don't think there is any place for them in the world. But the more of us who succeed, the more examples there will be for others.

If the white world thinks Native kids are worthless, then the best answer we can give them is to become the best — the best athletes, the best scholars, the best lawyers, the best parents — whatever. Not for them. For ourselves. To protect ourselves from all those negative messages.

Athletics has forced me to take school more seriously. I'm determined to get an athletic scholarship to university. Schools have already approached my coach about me — Florida State, Columbia University, University of Buffalo, University of Nebraska.

My ultimate goal is the Olympics, of course. After that, some sort of police work. Aboriginal communities need good police officers who know them and won't shoot them. And we can also use more women in the police.

To other kids, Aboriginal or not, I'd say, Get out there and run! Remember what it was like to be a little kid, when we just ran and ran because it was fun? You don't have to lose that feeling forever. Get out and run around and feel that joy again.

Jamie, 16

American Indians have a higher percentage of enrollment in the armed services than any other group. The first Native American recipient of the Medal of Honor (1869) was Co-Rux-Te-Chod-Ish, or Co-Tux-A-Kah-Waddle, who served with the Indian Scouts. In World War I, a law was passed requiring all Native American men to register for the draft even though they were not considered citizens and could not vote. Many thousands voluntarily joined the military. Many others protested this law. In Utah, for instance, the protests were so vehement that the army was called in to stop them.

More than 44,000 Native Americans served in World War II, where Navajo Code Talkers played a pivotal role. Ten thousand served in Korea and 42,000 in Vietnam. Ten thousand of those who have served have been women. Eighteen thousand have been sent to

Iraq or Afghanistan. First Nations people in Canada have also served with great distinction.

In Canada, Aboriginal veterans were for a long time not entitled to the same benefits granted to soldiers of European descent. Native veterans were told that since they were not considered Canadian citizens (First Nations people did not obtain the right to vote until 1960), they were not eligible for veterans' benefits. And it wasn't until 1992 that Aboriginal vets were allowed to lay a wreath at the National War Memorial in Ottawa on Remembrance Day.

At powwows, veterans are treated with special respect, and a ceremonial dance is done in their honor. Jamie and his sister, Sheila (shown in the photo), live in Iqaluit.

My sister is in grade nine. Her best subjects are math and science, and mine are math and English. I'm in grade ten. For a while, it looked like we were going to live in Coral Harbour. Mom started dating a guy from there a little while back, so we went and stayed there for a bit. It's on the south shore of Southampton Island, which is in the northern part of Hudson Bay.

I liked it there. It's really small with lots of wildlife. You used to be able to see caribou all the time in Iqaluit, but not anymore. We saw polar bear in Coral Harbour and caribou and fox. There's walrus and Beluga whales. It was easy to get to know everyone. Also there are no bars in Coral Harbour, so there were no drunk people around. I liked that a lot.

But it didn't work out with Mom's boyfriend, so we came back to Iqaluit. My mother's home community is here. Our dad's in Pangnirtung but now he's living somewhere in Ontario. Ottawa, I think. He sends us letters sometimes, but I don't know his address.

My sister and I are in foster care now. Our foster mom works at a bank. If people need a loan, they go talk to her. Our foster dad is a lawyer.

Our mother is here in Iqaluit but she's not well. She has a little problem with alcohol. She gets sad from all the things that have happened to her. So it's not good for us to live with her just now.

Our grandmother was the one who told us that we should join air cadets. I've been in it for about three years, my sister for two.

In cadets we learn all about flying, about planes, about survival, about the military. We do drills, shoot rifles, although we use pellets instead of real bullets.

We shoot at targets. There are different kinds. The one I like the best is where you shoot at different colors of dots. Another is a drawing of dynamite and you shoot at where the fuse lights up.

We have shooting competitions — cadets against the parents. Two cadets and two parents go on the shooting range, and they have to see who can hit the most targets in a certain amount of time.

We go to cadet camp in the summer in Whitehorse. The first year I went, I got to fly in two small planes. The planes have two pilots and three passengers. The cadet flies the plane along with the real pilot.

The basic cadet camp is in Whitehorse. After that I went to a basic leadership camp in Penhold, Alberta. Sheila and I went to the same camps for the first years, but this year she's going to a camp that teaches basic aviation and engineering. I'll be going to a six-week leadership training.

I've done some leadership training already. It teaches you how to get to know who your students are — who is quiet, who talks a lot, who learns fast, who learns better in groups. The idea is to learn how to teach things in a way that everyone can learn it and to also have fun while they're learning. At last year's camp we had to create our own teaching materials and decide how to do it.

You can learn survival training if you go to a basic survival training camp, but there's a big difference between survival in the south and survival up here in the north. Some things are the same but not many. How to build a fire, how to get help, how to get food. They're all different up here.

Drilling was hard to learn at first because it's not a regular way of moving. You have to concentrate. And if you're looking to the person in front of you to help you and they're not in step, then you're thrown off too.

But drilling is good because it teaches you how to discipline yourself and how to stay still. Often when you sit in the regular way, you fidget, or squirm, or your attention goes. It's hard to sit still and focus yourself. Try it and see. But it gets easier with practice. Our elders know how to do it. They had to do it during hunting and fishing.

When the training gets hard, I remind myself of all the opportunities we're getting. Sheila was thinking of quitting but decided to keep on with it. Next year she can get a glider's license if she works hard. That's a good deal.

The things Sheila doesn't like are putting gel in her hair to keep it smooth when she's in her uniform. I hate polishing my boots and I have to cut my hair every week. But I like the uniform and what I'm learning, and the good is more than the not so good.

We have a new officer leading us. She's tough and smart

Downtown Iqaluit.

and strong. She's giving us inspections every week. The cadet who has the best uniform gets free canteen. That means they get to choose some items from the canteen. It's snacks.

Sheila and I work at the Northern store. That's the big store here that sells groceries, clothes, furniture and camping gear. Sheila stacks groceries and carries heavy stuff. I work at a cash register. It's usually the other way around, with girls working the cash and guys doing stock. I've been working there for almost two years. I'd like to get a job at the Quick Stop variety store on the road to Apex. It's a smaller shop.

Iqaluit is a really good place, lots of homes and our school is really nice. But there are problems too. There's not a lot of shops, so if you don't like the clothes in the Northern store, you're kind of out of luck. Unless you're able to go south to shop, and a flight south is really expensive. It seems like almost every parent has to give up their kids or put their kids in foster care. Lots of kids don't have money to eat every day.

My supervisor at the Northern store told me to watch out for stealers. It puts me in a funny position because I don't want to get fired but I also don't want to get people in trouble. Most of the poor people are Inuit, not white. I don't want to rat on my own people. Some of the folks I've seen steal things I know are really poor, and they steal because they're hungry. One guy stole a box of frozen pizza. Another guy stole a bag of brown sugar. I guess it's what they could grab. Food is really expensive up here, and if you don't have a good job, it's easy to go hungry.

There are a lot of Inuit up here. More Inuit than white people, so I haven't had to deal with racism up here. There were times with other cadets when I went to camps in the south. One white kid used to talk to me as though I was stupid. This was at the camp in Penhold. I wasn't the only one he treated badly. The leaders caught on to this kid and he got RTU — Returned to Unit.

In my sister's flight — an air cadet word for group — a few white kids would ask her to say words in our language, then they'd make fun of how it sounded and say disrespectful things about our family. The flight sergeants made them knock it off.

Both my sister and I want to join the military when we're older. Sheila's also thinking about becoming a commercial pilot. We're learning things in cadets that will help us get there.

Angelica, 11

During the Second World War, the government took nearly one million acres from Native Americans for military purposes. Some of the land was used for training. Some of the land was used for Japanese internment camps.

The Western Shoshone have the unfortunate distinction of being the most heavily bombed nation on earth. Their land, which traditionally stretched from Idaho to California's Mojave Desert, includes the Nevada Test Site, where 928 American and 19 British atomic bombs have been detonated. Some were underground in a series of artificial tunnels and caves. Many were above ground.

Communities could feel the ground shake from the explosions and see the bright flashes of light. The radioactive dust settled on their homes, turning gardens black, killing animals and causing cancer in people.

The Duckwater Shoshone Tribe, in the high Nevada desert, was one of the communities contaminated by the fallout from these bombs.

I met Angelica in the community's gymnasium.

There are thirteen students in my school — the whole school. It's the Duckwater Shoshone Elementary School, and if you want to see it just walk out of this gym and go down the hall and it's right there.

We have two classrooms and a library. The thirteen of us are split into groups, all ages in each group, so we all study to-

Road to the Duckwater Shoshone Reservation.

gether. One teacher takes a group for reading, another takes a group for math, then we switch classrooms.

A year ago we had really bad scores on our reading tests. The teacher said, "I'll work really hard to help you all read better, and if you work really hard too, then we'll all be in it together." So we talked about it and decided that's what we would do. So we did.

I grew up here so it's normal for me to go to a small school. I went to another school for a while — the one up on the highway. It's a public school, so white kids go there. It's about the same size as this school. I like it here because I get to learn the Shoshone language.

There's a really big kitchen in this place, big like in a restaurant. Almost every week there is some event here and people from the community come and we all have a big meal together. We all know everyone and they all know us, and when someone asks us how we're doing in school we better have a good answer!

Today we're doing our Veterans' Day ceremony. Everyone is here. The whole rez. You could drive through the whole rez today and you wouldn't see anyone. Because they're all here! Even the kids from the other school are here.

I'm doing a Fancy Shawl Dance at the ceremony and I'm helping to give out the honors. All the kids in the school are taking part. Some are flag bearers. Some are dancers.

It's about honoring the veterans. We do it every year. Lots of people from here have been in the military. My mom was in the air guard for six years. In my family there are people who were in the marines and the air force. Almost everyone here has done that or had a relative who has done that.

What will happen is we'll have a grand entry. The dancers will come in, then the flags, and everyone will stand. Then the people who had people go to war will come forward and be honored. Then the people who went to war will come up and everyone applauds.

My great-granddad was in the army. He trained mine dogs — dogs that sniff out bombs in the ground. One of my teachers is a veteran too. It's a common thing.

My mom works at the planning office on the reservation. She has an office here, but she travels all over for her work. I go with her a lot and we meet other Native people. We go to Phoenix, Reno, Salt Lake City, all over. Mom has her meeting and I hang out with the other kids. It's good.

I have four sisters and two brothers, all older than me. Some are in their thirties. One of my sisters is in high school in Las Vegas. She's staying there with a friend. When the time comes for me to go to high school I'll bus out to Eureka probably, but I might stay here and do it online.

My house is out by itself, out by an old cattle car. There are lots of things I like to do in my free time. Play tag. Run around. I like basketball. I like baking pies. Last winter I made pies practically every day, I liked it so much. I may become a baker after I finish school. One of my favorite things is to swing from the tree branch in the yard. It makes the dogs bark and it's really funny.

We live out by Duckwater Falls, where the hot spring is. It's a big swimming hole and it's warm water all year round. You can just go for a swim even in the winter.

Duckwater isn't a big place and there's not a lot of people. We kids all know each other. When we have problems we have to work it out because we're all just here together.

Wusto, 15

The legacy of residential schools and colonialism has led many to try to mask their pain with alcohol and illegal drugs. While many reserves and reservations have been declared by their communities to be "dry" (no alcohol can be brought in or sold), smugglers still find ways to bring it in. New mining opportunities — including the building of roads and an influx of non-community workers — create new opportunities for smugglers.

I met Wusto at a Native youth drug treatment center.

I was born in Toronto but I grew up on Wikwemikong Reserve on Manitoulin Island. We call it Wiky for short. Mom is Ojibwe and my dad is Mi'kmaq.

I've lived most of my life in Wiky. It feels free up there. You can walk around late at night without being afraid. Little kids play all over the roads because there aren't many cars.

On the down side you can wake up on summer nights to the sound of people fighting. There's lots of drinking up there. Some adults go on week-long drinking binges.

It's a good place to live from birth until grade four, but not so good after that. There's very little for kids to do. That's why we end up drinking and on drugs.

After grade four, everything changes. You see older kids. You look up to them and want to do what they do.

The teachers don't say anything if they know you're high because if they kicked out all the kids in class who were high there'd be no one left in the classroom.

I went to school high on drugs every day in grade eight and no one said anything to me about it. The teachers could recognize the signs. It's not hard to spot.

I started out with weed, like everyone else. It's everywhere up there. After weed most kids move on to pills like Oxy-Contin and Percocet. Lots start oxys even younger than me. Oxys are hard to get off of. You get the shakes bad.

A friend's mom goes to Sudbury, the closest big city, and steals things. She sells what she steals and uses the money to buy drugs. Before her trip she goes to her customers and asks them what they want. She'll steal what they want, they'll pay her, and that's how she gets money.

In another friend's house there were ten kids, all getting high. Their dad's off somewhere, disappeared, and their mom says nothing. She grows weed in her basement. It brings in money.

If someone is getting investigated, someone in the police station will let the family know they're being watched. So it never ends.

There are often drug busts in the high school. The high school on the reserve is really nice. You can study Native languages there. But still, lots of drugs.

OxyContin is a prescription drug. It's for pain if you break a bone or something. People work at places where they can steal it, then sell it. It's expensive. It can cost you $30 to get high. The price goes up with the dosage.

I did oxy only once, but I'd do it again if I wasn't here in treatment. You crush the pill into tinfoil, light it and inhale the smoke. You get high as soon as you inhale. It's also called

Hillbilly Heroin. Once you breathe it in you just put your head back and be high. Your face feels happy.

Wiky could be a great place to live if it weren't so messed up. People my grandmother's age were sent to residential schools. They were taken away from their families, put into institutions, were punished for speaking their languages, were told they were no good because they're Indian. They lost touch with their families. A lot of them were hit or were sexually abused by the priests or teachers. When they grew up and got out and had their own kids, they had no idea how to be parents.

It wasn't just my grandparents' generation that this happened to. My dad had a terrible time at school too. He got hurt and picked on all the time by the white teachers, him and the other Native kids. He got picked up by the ears and dropped to the floor. They made him kneel on hot radiators. And he wasn't allowed to speak his language.

Alcohol was an escape. When Dad was a kid his mom and dad would be passed out on the floor and he'd take a taste of their booze. They made their own booze so it was cheap and always around. His parents were both in residential school. They didn't know how to be parents. They didn't know how to show him love.

There were lots of suicides in Dad's community when he was younger. There still are but they're trying to fix it.

Dad had a drinking problem for a long while, but he managed to get out of that cycle. He's been sober now for fifteen years.

It was in the summer between grade four and grade five that I first smoked grass. My friend and I found my brother's pipe that had some weed in it and we smoked that.

You don't need an actual pipe though. You can get an old

can, poke some holes in it and smoke weed through that.

I won't lie to you. There's parts about taking drugs that I really like. But there's parts I don't like too, like seeing what people are like after a lot of years of doing it. I've seen too many fights, too many wasted people.

I've always known that I'm going to college. My mom constantly tells me that I'm going and the way she says it, there's no arguing with her. Other people say I'll end up pregnant, on welfare and dead-ending it. My mom's voice is stronger. My mom is a woman you don't want to mess with. If she says I'm going to college, then I'm going. End of story.

Most kids don't have someone like my mom who will say things like that to them. And if you don't see anything different, you don't know there's anything different out there.

So I always knew I wasn't going to stay on drugs, but that didn't mean I was really ready to come off them now.

Mom and Dad were going to send me here in January but I said I could quit on my own. But I didn't quit. So one morning, early, they woke me up and said, "You're going to treatment." I refused. They said, "We're your parents. We're making you go."

I've had a few little problems with the law. I was on probation already for theft. I took my mom's car without asking her and my aunt called the cops. I also have driving without a license, break and enter, and I've gotten warnings for disturbing the peace, being intoxicated in public and trespassing.

The night I got the warnings I also got bottled. Someone threw a bottle at me during a fight. So I got a big bruise.

So, between my parents and the police, I was pretty much forced to come here. But it's been mostly good, really good. I've learned a lot about myself and about my culture. I feel ready to leave old things behind and start a new life.

I'm still aiming for college or university. For sure I'll take Native languages and Native studies. Beyond that I'm not sure. Maybe architecture.

The bottom line is that Native people are really amazing and strong and beautiful and can do a lot of things when they have something to believe in.

Brad, 17

According to the Death Penalty Information Center, Native Americans are put in prison at a rate that's 38 percent higher than the national rate. In Canada Aboriginals make up 4 percent of the population but 23 percent of inmates, up from 17 percent ten years ago. Native prisoners are also more likely to be sent to maximum security or segregation, and prison guards are more likely to use force on them than on white inmates. A relationship has been established between dropping out of high school and being put behind bars. Racism also plays a big role. According to the Native Women's Association of Canada, 40 percent of Aboriginal inmates in Canadian prisons are either residential school survivors or they are the children of survivors or they were affected by the Sixties Scoop. Many become reoffenders.

In recent years, much work has been done to create opportunities for restorative justice — the sort of justice that brings healing to both the victim and the perpetrator, helping to ensure that the offender will not offend again. But too many young people are still caught up in the old system that focuses on punishment.

I met with Brad inside a youth prison.

I'm from Hamilton. I never met my grandparents. Just my mom and brothers and sisters. Dad left when I was two or three. Mom is a single mom. She doesn't have a job.

We're Mohawk. My mom's family is from the Six Nations

reserve. My dad's family is from the reserve too. I haven't had any contact with them. When I was younger it didn't matter. Now that I'm older I'd like to see my dad again and meet my other relatives. I don't know if I'll get to do that or not.

I've been in this youth prison for a year. I get out in a couple of weeks.

I've been in and out of custody since I was twelve. I've been in four closed prisons and lots of open-custody places. Open custody means no fence and you go on lots of outings. The YMCA will take you out to movies, things like that.

I've been charged with different things over the years. Two frauds, four assaults with a deadly weapon, assault causing bodily harm, identity theft. Things like that.

I only met my mom a couple of years ago. I knew her when I was a lot younger of course, but I don't remember. Children's Aid took me into foster care when I was four.

I grew up in foster homes. A lot of foster homes. You're always nervous at first because you don't know the people and you want to say the right thing so they won't hate you.

I was in one foster home for a few years. They liked me and wanted to adopt me. But then one of their other foster kids hit their daughter. I pushed him down the stairs to get him away from her. The daughter didn't speak up for me, so it looked like I was just a bad kid, and they threw me out.

After that it was a lot of foster homes and a lot of group homes. None of the foster parents were Native. Some were white, some were Jamaican. Native parents raise their kids different. It's a different rhythm. More patience and under-standing, less giving out orders and punishments.

I've been in six different group homes.

The group homes were awful. I would never want to go back to one of those places again. They're dirty. All my stuff

Fence surrounding the youth prison.

got stolen. The kids who end up in group homes are the ones that are rejects from foster homes. They're the kids everyone has given up on. They're like waiting rooms for jails because no one expects anything worthwhile of us so they don't put anything worthwhile into us.

I finally found my mom again a few years ago. She's been an addict for a long time, smoking crack and taking pills. She's been clean for a year. I told her, "I'll love you no matter what, but if you don't stop doing drugs you'll never be able to see us." So she stopped, but it wasn't easy. Addictions are hell. She goes now to a methadone clinic and has to give regular urine samples to prove she's clean.

She had a terrible life. She's been stabbed, raped, beaten by a man using a bat with spikes on it. When she was a kid she was raped by her own dad. He was a prison guard. At another prison, not here, a prison for adults. All the other guards there knew he did it. None of them did anything to help my mother. She said he told her how he bragged about it to them. She got pregnant from him. He took her to get the abortion.

I'm in here now because I stabbed another guy who also raped my mom.

I never used the rape as my defense. I never told the court that's why I did it. I figured that was my mother's story to tell, not mine. I just kept silent and took my punishment. I'm really protective of my family. I've stabbed a lot of people — guys, that is, not women. It's always guys who are hurting other people. I've never been hurt by a woman. I stabbed a guy who was kicking my sister, stabbed another guy who was beating another sister. I never use that as a defense.

I do get nervous going to court, even though I've been there a lot. If you're already in custody, they take you from jail to the central police station and they put you in a cell. To take you up to court they put shackles and handcuffs on you. You sit like that for a while in the courthouse cells. It's boring and uncomfortable. If you get fed, it's crap food, the cheapest thing they can find. And if it's moldy, so what? You're nothing. They make sure you know it. Then they bring you into the court, the adults talk for a while, then they take you back to the cell again.

Sometimes they'll let me talk. The judge might ask, "Are these the facts?" Sometimes they'll ask you for an explanation, but if you say one thing slightly different from what the lawyer already said, that causes more trouble and more delays, so what's the point of saying anything?

Court is not a natural environment for a kid. A kid just wants to talk and have a conversation, but court is not a place where you feel comfortable to do that. I get that we're there because we're in trouble and it's set up so that we feel intimidated. I just don't think it really solves any problems.

I've got fourteen high-school credits. There's a school at this prison. It's good to be able to study. I've got a job waiting for me when I get out of here, roofing and welding. And I'm going to learn drywalling. I hope I can finish school, but we'll have to see.

The longest I've ever been in custody is two and a half years. It really feels weird to get out of prison and see that everyone you know has gotten older. You've been locked away in a time capsule and the world has gone on without you.

This is a prison, so there are hard things, but there are good things too. I think they think that because we're young, there might still be a chance we can turn things around, that we're not hard-core criminals yet. So we go to classes, there's a weight room, there's a yard where we can play basketball, there's a library.

We're on a strict schedule. We wake up at 6:30, shower, go to breakfast, brush our teeth and do our chores. Everyone does their chore then goes back to their room until the chores are all done. We're assigned chores like cleaning the washrooms and showers, mopping the floor, cleaning the lounge. We do them morning and evening.

After chores we go to school for seventy-five minutes, back to the cells for a count, then another seventy-five minutes of school. After lunch we have a twenty-minute break. Then it's school, break, school again. By that time it's 3:30.

Then we have activities. Sometimes it's swimming or weights or in the gym or outside. You go with your range. You don't have to go. You can stay in your cell, but if you go, you go with the range.

There have been lots of scraps among the guys lately. Lots

of fighting with the corrections officers. Sometimes it's calm here for a long time. Then it changes and for weeks everyone is getting insulted and fighting back.

Some COs treat you really good, like they actually care about how you're doing. Others just look at it as a job.

If you break the rules they send you to your cell. Sometimes they put you on twenty-four-hour lock-down where you have to stay in your cell on your stool. You can't move, you can't read. You just sit there. They watch you through the window.

Sometimes they put you in the hole, in solitary. I just got out of solitary, just before I came down here to talk to you. Solitary cells have a metal bed with a thin mat and a horse blanket. There's a painted-over window in a cage, a metal toilet and a hatch in the door for the food tray.

There are six cells in the solitary wing. If there are three or more kids in the cells, a guard stays in the wing. If there are less than three, a guard comes in to check on you every half hour. If you don't talk to them, they won't talk to you.

You're in there all the time. You can have a Bible and sometimes other books, but nothing else. The longest I've done in solitary is a month. I thought I was going crazy.

I hit two guards. That's why they threw me in there this last time.

I think I'll be institutionalized when I get out of here. I can cook, but only a little. I don't know anything about how to conduct my life, like how to use a bank, things like that. I'm going to have to catch up.

I don't feel like I'm a part of any society. Not Native society, not Canadian society. Nothing. I'm a person on the outside.

Kristin, 17

The Pueblo Indians of the American Southwest possess a culture unique in the North American landscape. Some of the homes they carved out of the sandstone cliffs were five stories high and had hundreds of rooms. Taos Pueblo is a designated UNESCO World Heritage Site and also a National Historic Landmark.

Today there are nineteen pueblos in New Mexico, each with its own history, cultural practices and artistic traditions. There used to be ninety-nine. Francisco Vásquez de Coronado of Spain, credited with "discovering" the Grand Canyon, came through the area on his search for the legendary Seven Cities of Gold. He massacred whole families in 1540, tying people to stakes and burning them alive. Eighty pueblos were destroyed, never to be rebuilt.

The Southwest is also known as the place where the United States government tested the atomic bomb. Much of the uranium for those bombs came from a massive open-pit uranium mine on the Laguna Pueblo, causing long-term health problems for the people. While the pit is still there, the Laguna people are working to reclaim it.

The Acoma Pueblo, where Kristin works, is also known as Sky City because of the ancient and still-inhabited city on top of the mountain. The three hundred homes there are owned by the women who, by tradition, pass them on to their youngest daughters.

I've been involved with the Ancestral Lands project for three years. I was sort of forced into it to start with. I kept running away from home, having troubles with the law. I don't like to talk about the details of that. It's in the past, and I've fixed up all the things that I did wrong.

But I will say that I was sent to a lot of places by the court system. Some of the places were not too bad, and the people who ran them tried to make them fun. After all, we were kids. We were in trouble, but we were still kids.

Some of the places they put me in were really hard. They locked me up and I hated that. I was trapped.

The court referred me to this project because I had to do some community service hours. I stayed for a while, kind of testing it out, seeing what the people were like. They seemed good, but I'm not used to things going well. I ran away again in the middle of it because I was sure it would not continue to be good. It was going to turn bad somehow and I didn't want to be there when it did. Then I kind of kicked myself and thought, what if this time I was wrong? Then I decided to ask to come back and give it another try.

I see the program as an opportunity to fix the mistakes I made in the past. I finished all the court-ordered stuff last summer and decided to stay with it.

The director, Cornell, talks to us a lot about consequences. He says our actions should reflect our values, that sure we could spend our paychecks on booze and drugs, but there are consequences to doing that, and what does that tell the world about who we are if we make that choice?

Desert around Acoma Pueblo.

He talks to us and we talk to each other. It helps us stay strong and on the right path.

A kid will come back from the weekend and say, "I almost got into a car with my buddies even though I knew they were going drinking and were using drugs. But I didn't. Three hours after I left them, they got busted by the cops. They're sitting in jail this morning, and I'm back at work!"

Cornell started this project because he and his wife came home from the casino at 2:30 one morning. He saw two thirteen-year-old girls running around, and in his mind he saw his own daughters. He didn't want children leading lives like that. He wanted kids to have the opportunity to become something.

Ancestral Lands is part of the Southwest Conservation Corps. It has lots of youth programs. They work with Pueblo youth, Navajo, Hopi. All Native youth. As Native Americans, we're taught to respect the earth, but modern culture makes us forget that. The corps has a hiking club for younger kids ten to thirteen. The kids get backpacks, compasses and water bottles — things they need on a hike. They go on hiking trips out on the ancestral land. They meet with archeologists, elders, national park people. Gives them an idea that there's a big world out there, bigger than watching TV or playing video games.

The preservation crew, which is what I'm on, is for older youth. We look after the natural areas. Sometimes we cut down trees that are not indigenous to our area. Someone or something has brought them in from someplace else. They drink up a lot of water, which means the local plants don't get what they need. I've spent a lot of time clearing cactus out of a canyon just south of Acoma. We clear away cactus and other invasive plants and in their place we plant natural local grasses which give the wildlife something to eat.

There's usually fourteen on a team, and we work hard! The work we do helps preserve and clean the water in the canyon. Our ancestors lived on this land. It belongs to us and we want to pass it on to the next generation in good shape.

We all wear yellow hardhats and gray T-shirts, and we start every day with exercises like push-ups to get our muscles ready for the work ahead. Every time there's a decision to be made or information to be shared, we form a circle so everyone can feel they can be seen and heard. It's also so that it's clear we're all in this together.

I love coming in to work in the morning. We laugh every day! Sometimes I don't even want to leave work to go home. We're all here to do a job, and we know that the job is important, and we take that seriously, but we can also have a lot of fun.

Traditional pueblo oven.

Struggling with cactus is really hard. You have to be careful not to get hurt or hurt your teammates.

Picking up trash means more plants will grow and the soil will be healthier. Clearing out moss and things from the water means the water will flow better. It might even get clean enough one day that people can just drink right from the river, the way we used to.

We've learned how to work together to make a job go easier. And kids who have never made real friends in their lives have made good friends here. During lunch we put all the food we've brought from home in the middle of the circle. Some kids come with no food. Not because they're lazy but because there's no food in their house. If we pool what we have, then everybody eats, and there's enough for everyone.

I'm much healthier and stronger now than I was when I started, even though I thought I was tougher. There's something really special about taking a place that's ugly and making it beautiful. The first project I worked on, we fixed up a playground that was in bad shape. We painted it, repaired it, cut down weeds, picked up the trash. We made it safe for the little kids. I feel real proud even now when I see kids playing on it.

And the river I'm helping to clear — when I'm an elder I'll take all the little kids in the community out to see it and tell them all about how I helped clean it up. You really feel it's your land if you sweat a little to take care of it.

We cannot give up our rights without destroying ourselves as a people. If our rights are meaningless ... then we as a people are meaningless. We cannot and we will not accept this.

— Harold Cardinal, Cree, from *The Unjust Society: The Tragedy of Canada's Indians*

Danielle, 18

According to Columbia Journalism School's Dart Center and Amnesty International, one in three Native American women will be sexually assaulted in her lifetime. In the general population, the rate is one in six. Most rape cases of Native women go unprosecuted. Eighty-five percent of the rapists of Native women are non-Native men, and tribal police forces have no legal ability to arrest white men.

The Native American Women's Health Education Resource Center has looked at the barriers Native Americans face in receiving health care, including contraception, leading women who get pregnant because of rape to be forced to give birth to the child of their rapist.

Programs to empower Indigenous women to keep themselves safe are growing popular. Women's self-defense courses on the Wind River Reservation in Wyoming and on the Fort Peck Reservation in Montana are just two examples.

But many Native American and Aboriginal women who report that they have been raped are still simply not believed.

That's what Danielle came up against.

I've lived here for about ten years. Before here, I lived in Timiskaming. But then Mom met someone she wanted to be with, and we moved here. My dad is German. I'm a non-status Native, an Algonquin from the Kipawa First Nation. I've lived in a few places, actually. I was even in foster care for a while.

I like doing the same things other young women my age do, like shopping, hanging out with friends. I work hard in school and get good grades. My best subjects are math and science.

The outside world is not so easy.

I work at a fast food place in the city. Dealing with customers is a real challenge. They'll yell at me because the taxes are too high! I don't set the taxes! I just bring them their burgers. The trick is to stay calm when people are yelling at you, so that you can feel you are in control.

I'm light-skinned. My skin is so light that my non-Native friends don't realize I'm Native. I don't come flat out and say I am. I just let them think what they want. I don't want the hassle of having to answer their questions, but it means I have to put up with anti-Native comments — not from my friends, but from their friends.

My mother wants nothing to do with white people. The world made her that way. She had it hard growing up. She went to a white school in North Bay and got bullied all the time for being Native. She'd get insulted, beaten up, shoved into walls and lockers. She hated being Native because she thought that was the root of all her problems. She turned her back on her heritage, got involved with a white guy, gave up her Native status. She wanted to be white so that she would be treated better. She learned though. Wanting to be white doesn't mean that the white world will accept you as one of their own.

I can get my Native status back through my grandfather. He's passed away now. I'm wearing his cardigan. He was taken away from his family when he was very young because the Canadian government didn't think that Native parents should raise their own children.

I got into drugs and alcohol when I was fifteen. My mom was going through a rough patch then, and she started hitting me, so I started acting out. I moved out to a friend's house. My friend was staying with her aunt who was an alcoholic, so you can imagine how that went. She got kicked out of her aunt's house, so then I had no place to go. I got put into foster care. I stayed there for nine months.

I was put into a foster home with another First Nations family, a single mom and her daughter. Really good people. I wasn't used to living in a calm place where people were nice to each other and things were predictable, like meals on time. It was different. It was good, but I wasn't used to it. My foster mom made me tell her where I was going and let her know if I was going to be late. That's a normal parent thing to do, but it was strange to me.

I had to leave the foster home because I was sexually assaulted. Not in the home, but in that general neighborhood. I went to the police about it, but the cops said I looked promiscuous and I was probably just claiming rape because I regretted a bad decision. I went to the women's shelter. They believed me and let me stay there for a while, but a shelter is not a home. I couldn't stay there forever.

Children's Aid put me in a group home for a few months. The people who ran it were okay, but it was a mixed group home, guys and gals. Why would they put a sexual assault survivor in a group home with guys? There need to be more safe homes for young women.

All of that is behind me now. I don't waste a bit of time looking backward.

Being Native is an important part of who I am, even though I don't talk about it a lot. I believe in the Creator and in having respect for the earth.

I live on my own now, in a little apartment. It's good I feel safe there, and it gives me lots of quiet to do my school work. I'm now in a school where it's considered cool to study and succeed. Imagine that. I'm in the cool group!

In the future I'm hoping to be a sexual assault counselor. I'm writing a book about my experience, about what I went through and the things others did that made it worse.

I struggle not to be a downer. I don't want to think negative thoughts. The Creator has given us a wonderful world, full of beautiful things. When we have a positive outlook, we honor what the Creator has done.

Cheyenne, 9

The horse has been an integral part of Indigenous culture ever since it arrived in North America in the 1500s. The Spanish, who brought the horses to North America from their battles in Central America and Mexico, originally made it against the law for Native Americans to ride a horse. In 1680, Pueblo Indians chased the Spanish out of New Mexico, keeping their horses. Horses spread from there into many other tribes.

For community members who suffered through the ravages of residential school abuses, horses have provided a grounding in traditional beliefs and values. The Smithsonian Institution's exhibit, A Song for the Horse Nation, looks at the connections between horses and Indigenous people.

Cheyenne is doing her part to continue the tradition of respect.

I've just started fourth grade. I go to a Montessori school in Alpine, Texas. It's a small town, but I don't live in town. I live on a four-hundred-acre ranch with my mother, Rachael Waller, who is a wild horse photographer, and my dad, Rod Rondeaux, who is an actor and does stunt riding in the movies. He was in over forty movies, like *Cowboys and Indians*, *Into the West* and *Meek's Cutoff*. He's away a lot because he gets a lot of jobs. But he comes home when he can.

I've always loved horses. And horses can tell when somebody loves them.

When I was really small, just a baby, my dad was holding me. Mom was going to take a picture of us. Up walked my father's stallion, Roach. He came right over to me and put his head near me to say hello, and his head was bigger than my whole body was then! Roach liked to avoid most people. But he came right up to me as if he knew that I was his and he was mine.

I've been riding horses ever since then. I have fifteen horses including Roach. Dad gave him to me a long time ago. The mare I ride most came from an auction. She was pregnant and if nobody wanted her they were going to send her to be slaughtered.

Three of my horses came from the Nebraska 200. A terrible man named Jason had two hundred horses. He was starving them and not giving them enough water. Someone reported him and all his horses were taken away from him. Sixty of them were too sick and they died. He went to court and even got sent to jail. Now he can never have another animal, not as long as he lives.

I don't know why he treated them so badly. He didn't need to do that. If he didn't want his horses anymore, he could have given them away instead of starving them.

So I have three of his horses. One of them is named Lazarus. This is an amazing story. Lazarus is from the Bible. It's someone they thought was dead but he stood up and wasn't dead. My horse, everyone thought he was dead. The vet had him on the table to look at him, and the vet said, "Put him outside. This one didn't make it." So they put him outside on the ground, but the horse decided he wasn't ready to be dead yet. He got up and surprised everyone. So they called him Lazarus, and he is one of my horses. And he can live the whole rest of his life in happiness and freedom, with no more torture and being scared.

My pony, Dancer, is going blind in both eyes. He runs into stuff. When I ride him I'm his eyes, and then he's fine.

I have a donkey too. Her name is Penelope. She likes peppermints, carrots and apples. She's got a good nature if you're kind to her, but if you try to be rude to her she'll go all stubborn and refuse to do anything. We found her on Freecycle. com. Her previous owners couldn't care for her anymore, so they found her a good home with us.

Mom and I went on a trip a little while ago to see the wild horses in northern New Mexico, by the Jicarilla Apache Reservation and Carson National Forest. Our friend Lynne Pomeranz went with us. She did a book called *Among Wild Horses*. It was a picture-taking holiday. Mom's teaching me about photography. We saw two stallions fighting and I was the only one who got the shot.

What can I say about wild horses? They're amazing. They are my favorite animal and I love them dearly. The mothers are very protective of their children, and the babies will come right up to you and smell you. I love watching them play and have fun.

And they are living the way they are supposed to live, running free. But they are being rounded up all the time. Sometimes they are even shot by helicopters. When Mom told me about what was happening I decided to do something about it. I want to be able to still see wild horses running around when I'm really old.

I started out doing drawings on posters about it. Then I did a drawing that my mom found a way to put on T-shirts. So now we sell the T-shirts. We have a web page on Facebook. We've raised over a thousand dollars for wild horse rescue.

There are so many things I like to do. My parents taught me to drive their Toyota pick-up truck. I don't drive it on the roads of course, but the ranch is a big place. Sometimes I take the truck down to the stream where the horses like to drink, just so I can watch them. Sometimes I drive the truck while my mother sits in the back and tosses out hay to the horses. When I'm not doing that and when I'm not in school, I do martial arts and Tahitian dancing.

I'm in a documentary film too. It's called *She Had Some Horses*, and it's about women and horses and feeling better.

My father is a full-blood Crow Indian. My mom is a mixture of a lot of tribes, so that makes me Sioux, Cheyenne and Crow. But my nation is the Crow nation.

My father was born in Los Angeles. The government sent Indians to live in cities, so his mom was there. She worked in a court house. When Dad was six months old, his grandmother came and took him back to the reservation so that he could grow up there. His reservation was the Crow Reservation. It was where the Pryor Mountain Wild Mustang Center is, so I've been around horses a lot, even before I was born.

My ceremonial uncle was Floyd Red Crow Westerman. He was an actor and was in a lot of movies like *Dances with Wolves* and a lot of others. He took me to my first sweat lodge. I prayed very hard when he was sick, but he still died. He taught me a lot of things, like how to pray and how to burn sage. It's real quiet out here, so I have lots of time to think about things.

There's lots more I want to know. My dad is going to teach me how to speak his language. English is his third language. Before he knew English he spoke Cheyenne and Sioux.

I want to spend all my life around horses. When I get older, I'll either be a horse trainer or a big cat specialist. There's a lot I can do, and when I get older, there will be even more things to do.

Cheyenne's Wild Horse and Burro Fund is on Facebook.

Rose, 12

The General Allotment Act of 1887 — also known as
the Dawes Act — was a law that was supposed to
eliminate whatever was left of Native cultures in the
United States. It called for reservation lands to be divided into plots on which individual families would
farm and make a living. Once all the plots were handed out, the rest of the land was sold to whites. Everything was managed by the Bureau of Indian Affairs.
The goal was to end government responsibility for
providing what it had agreed to under treaties (such
as rations, medical care and education), and to free
up lots of land for white settlers.

At the time the act was passed, Native American
land totaled over 250,000 square miles. Fifty-three
years later when the act was repealed, less than one-
quarter of that was still considered Native territory.

Darla Thiele still lives on land plotted out to her

ancestors by the Dawes Act. On it she runs a program called Bringing Back the Horses, which trains at-risk youth in the skills of horseback riding. Part equine education, part cultural centering and part life-skills training, the program gives kids confidence, strength and a sense of their own amazing abilities.

I met with Rose on Darla's land on the Spirit Lake Indian Reservation in North Dakota.

All the horses here have different personalities. Sundance is the Appaloosa an FBI agent gave to us. Sundance is stubborn. Diamond is brown with a white stripe on the nose. Diamond is the best listener. Lily is a paint. She likes to show off. She jumped a fence once! Lily will let kids get on her back — even beginners — but she doesn't like adults and she throws most of them off. And Jack is a horse that everybody likes. The problem with Jack is that a man came here who wasn't supposed to and took Jack out for a ride and treated him badly, so we're not riding Jack for a while, not until he trusts us again and isn't hurting from what happened to him.

The horse who thinks he's the boss of everybody isn't a horse at all but a little Shetland pony named Ho Ho who chases the other horses around the field. He's always grouchy but I don't mind that.

I didn't know anything about horses when I started coming here. Our ancestors had horses. We are Dakota Sioux, and so we were horse people. Horses were everything to us. They could talk to us and we could talk to them. Kids would be the first ones to see the horses every morning, taking them food and water, and they would be the last to see them at night, making sure they were all right. So no one was afraid of the horses. They were a part of what was going on.

Some kids are so afraid of horses when they first come here they don't even want to look at the horse when they're grooming them, and if the horse sneezes, the kid screams! But they soon get over that. Horses are just good, and if there is a mean one, it's because someone has treated him badly.

We used to all know about horses, but the government didn't want the Sioux to be powerful, so a lot of what we knew got lost. But not forever lost.

Before we started working with the horses we had indoor time. We sat in the double-wide trailer and had lessons from Darla and Mr. Holy Bull about our history, our culture, lots of sacred things. It's not just about getting on a horse. We can't tell a horse what to do unless we really know who we are.

Getting on a horse isn't like getting in a car. If the horse doesn't want to go, it won't go. If it feels that you are mad or upset, it won't want you on its back. So you have to leave all that behind when you go up to a horse. Whatever happens at school or at home, if you have a bad day, you take that off and leave it on the ground when you go in the corral. There's you and there's the horse. The horse doesn't care if you are a millionaire.

When you first meet a horse, you're strangers. You have to take it slow. Get to know each other. It's great when the horse recognizes you.

The horses are mostly loose in the big meadow behind Darla's house, and we have to go and get them when it's time to ride. Sometimes a horse is not in the mood. They'll let you walk right up close then they'll run away. I'm pretty good at getting them to come to me. I go into the field and wait and they come trotting over to say hello.

Darla has a lot of rules we have to follow. You can't talk on a cell phone when you're on the horse. You can't be on drugs or booze. You are responsible for whatever horse you ride, for looking after the tack, for grooming, all that.

We do lots of games with the horses. Horses don't like it when they can't see. We blindfold them and Darla has us lead them around a sort of baseball diamond she makes in the corral. We have to talk softly to the horse and keep touching it gently so it will trust us and go with us. Then we talk about it — what the horse might be feeling and if we ever feel like that. Like, if the horse's ears are back, it's a sign he's afraid, and what do we do when we're afraid?

I live with my grandmother. I have other brothers and sisters, but they live in Fargo with my mother. I didn't want to move to Fargo because I wanted to stay here with the horses, so my grandmother said I could live with her. We live on the reservation. It's a big reservation, with some little towns, a casino, schools, churches, some stores, usual things.

I don't go to the Christian church. I'm a member of the Peyote Church. It's a Native American church. It's Native spirituality. We meet every month at the beginning of the month. The meetings are to celebrate our being here. We drink tea, eat medicine, sing and pray all night.

I was baptized into it when I was a baby, maybe two weeks old. It happened at sunrise. They shaped ashes to look like the horizon, then used sage leaves to make an X over it, then they burned the sage with some cedar, smudged everyone, including me! It's a blessing. We have rituals, prayers, sacred objects like beaded gourds and drums made out of animal skins. Things like that.

My dad is in prison. I had another sister and brother. Destiny was nine and Travis was six. They died. Dad was looking after them in the house in Saint Michael, a little village down the road from here. My dad was drinking a lot and they ended up dead. So he's in prison. I went to visit him there, when he was in jail in Rugby and again when he was sent to another jail.

It's not a nice thing, to see him there. I don't know when he's coming back. He used to work for the fire department. I don't know what he does in prison. I don't know what there is to do. Probably just sit.

Nothing's really changed with them gone. The rez is still the same old rez. But I don't like it when men drink too much. I was riding just down the lane from here when the horse decided to stop for a while and didn't feel like going again when I wanted it to. A drunk guy came up and started throwing stones at the horse to make it go. Then he pulled me right out of the saddle and got on the horse's back. The other girls had to run and get Darla. Darla was mad. She said he's a nice man when he's sober but does stupid things when he drinks. We had to give the horse a rest after that and Mr. Holy Bull smudged to take away the bad spirits of the drinking.

I come here every day, almost. Even if we don't ride there are things to do, things to take care of. Darla always has food for us. It's a special place. There's a little cemetery by the corral. Some of the people buried there are Darla's ancestors. Others are Native people that the Christian cemeteries wouldn't bury because the Christians didn't think the Natives were good enough.

Next week we're going to be part of a memorial ride with some Canadians. We'll be remembering a massacre that happened two hundred years ago. There will be lots of different tribes speaking lots of different languages. Dakota, Cree, Ojibwe. It's a four-day ride. We did a memorial ride for war veterans a few weeks ago.

You can't fool a horse. A horse knows if you're not a good person, if you're angry, if you're carrying a big lie. A horse also knows if you have respect, if you are trying to be brave and if you have a good heart. You can't fool a horse. A horse always knows the truth.

Eagleson, 17

The Ditidaht Nation is one of fourteen nations belonging to the Nuu-chah-nulth Tribe of the Pacific Northwest. It is a land of giant cedars. The original people used the cedars to build their homes, for dugout canoes and for totem poles. The tradition today continues in the city of Seattle, where Aboriginal carvers sit on benches in Victor Steinbrueck Park and create incredible works of art with a piece of wood and a pocket knife.

Eagleson is a young carver. He spoke with me from the carving shed on Seattle's waterfront.

I'm the eighth generation of woodcarvers in my family. I started into carving when I was three years old. My grandpa and my father inspired me.

My grandfather was blind, but he still carved. He felt the wood with his fingers and could see the design without actually seeing it. My father is Rick Williams and my mother is from the white community. They don't live together.

I'm in the tenth grade in school. My best subjects are history and math. I'm probably going to study mechanics. And keep carving, of course. I go to Indian Heritage School. They know I'm down here doing this carving and they let me set my own schedule.

The totem I'm working on is a seven-figure design. My

grandfather created the design in 1910. I'll come here and carve all day. I usually sleep here too.

Students come here to learn from me. I have seven students I teach about history and traditional painting techniques. I'm interested in learning how to make paint the way we did in the old days, bringing the colors from the natural world into the art we do. Paint can be made from fish eggs, flowers, bugs, rocks, shells, wood. All kinds of things. I want to learn more about that so I can teach it to others.

All ages of people come to the carving shed to watch and learn — older people and younger people. It takes a long time to learn. I've had my whole class come down here and check out the totems.

When it's done we're going to raise this totem and carry it from here to the Space Needle, where it will stand. Only Natives will carry it.

A lot of white people say they love Native culture. They say they love our work and love the way we look when we're all dressed up for powwows, but they don't really want us around as human beings. When we're not dancing or painting, I think they'd like us to just go away. They don't want to think about what their ancestors did to my ancestors, and what's still going on right now.

My uncle, John T. Williams, also a woodcarver, was shot and killed by a policeman. He was fifty years old and he was deaf. They shot him when he was walking down the street. He had a problem with alcohol, and was walking unsteady down the street, carrying a block of wood and a carving knife. The police knew him. They knew he was a good man, but they shot him and he died. They didn't think of him as a person. Maybe they looked at him and thought, oh, he's limping, his long hair isn't combed, his clothes are baggy, he's not important.

The carving knife he was carrying was just a three-inch pocket knife, the one he'd had forever. The blade wasn't even open. The cop yelled at him to stop, then seconds later shot him four times. He was on the ground dead, and the police still put him in handcuffs.

I'm doing this carving in my uncle's memory.

There's a lot of alcoholism in my family. I used to drink too. I started when I was twelve, and I kept it up for a long time. I was living with my mom then and just drank because — well, I just did. It wasn't good. It didn't make me feel good. It just made me feel like nothing. It even got boring after a while. I finally quit because my mom kicked me out. I live with my dad now, but really I mostly stay at the waterfront here 24/7.

Seattle has a lot of Native Americans. Many of them come from the reservations in the area. Some have lost their way and they do drugs and drink. They live on the pavement and people walk past them as if they are garbage. I'll sit and talk to them, try to talk them out of drinking. Or they'll find their way down to where I'm carving and they'll just sit, to be close to their culture, to something that's real.

When the carving was completed, ninety people carried the John T. Williams Memorial Totem Pole from Seattle's waterfront to the park by the Space Needle. It rises thirty-four feet into the air.

Nancie, 9, and Breanne, 13

Native royalty pageants are one way many communities honor the strong young women among them. Chosen for their knowledge of their nation and culture and for their confidence in sharing what they know with others, Native princesses are ambassadors for their nations.

Sisters Nancie and Breanne have both been involved in pageants. They are from the Chippewa Nation.

Nancie

My mother's name was Nancy with a *y*. I'm Nancie with an *ie*.

I live with my Aunt Jan. She was married to Uncle Ramy but he passed away from a heart attack. He was really funny. He always had jokes to tell and goofy random songs to sing, like "A Spoonful of Sugar." He'd just burst into singing it at any old time.

I used to have a sister. Her name was Ashley. She died a few months ago. She was seventeen. I don't know how she died. They won't tell me.

Ashley was fun and cool. She was a lot older than me, so she didn't want to always hang out with me. She had her own friends, but I had my own friends too! I like to go camping with my friend Abbey on the weekends, and Ashley liked to go out with her friends.

But she did hang out with me a lot. We didn't do anything special, just passed the time, went for walks to the park and things like that. We'd laugh and be silly. It always felt a little free, being out with her. She was usually nice to me. When she wasn't, it was just regular sister stuff, nothing big.

I have two brothers. My oldest one is especially funny. We have pretend fights. He pretends I've hurt him and then he fakes crying. It's really funny.

I'm not sure where my dad is. Mom comes to visit once a week, usually on Sunday, or I go to see her.

I like everything about school, especially gym. We play this game called Sharks and Fish. Three kids stand in the middle and they're the sharks. The other kids are fish. The sharks have to try to catch the fish. It's fun.

When I get older I want to help pets be healthy and be a teacher and have a shop called Fancie Nancie, full of cool clothes for girls.

At the powwows I'm a Jingle dancer. The dress jingles when it moves, and the sound and rhythm of it makes me happy. It was hard to learn the dance when I was younger. When you're just starting out your feet don't quite do what your mind tells them to do. But I kept at it and it's easy now.

I love doing really fancy steps. I love having lots of braids and beads in my hair. Some of the dancing outfits are really heavy from all the beads and decorations.

I design my own outfits. I love to use lots of color, lots of brightness. A friend of my aunt makes them. In my shop, Fancie Nancie, I'll sell a lot of clothes that I design. I do my own earrings too. One of my outfits for winter, is red, yellow, black and white. There's a blue and white one for the summer.

My sister Ashley loved dancing. She was powwow princess last year, and that's a big honor. You have to know a lot about being Chippewa and you have to be the sort of person others will look at and feel proud.

There's a junior princess and a senior princess. Ashley was the senior princess. Next year I'll be old enough to try to be junior princess.

Grief is really hard. I try to stay happy because there's a lot of happy things in my life, but sometimes I get very, very sad about my sister. When I get that really heavy sadness, the kind that makes my chest hurt, I go to one of my friends and ask her to cheer me up. She'll tell jokes and get me playing and then I can feel happy again.

Breanne

I'm in grade eight. My best subject is Ojibwe language because of the atmosphere in the classroom. Ojibwe classes are very relaxed and welcoming. We do language lessons and also learn about cultural things and stories of our history. It's like taking a deep, calm breath, going into that room. Even the pictures on the walls reflect who we are.

Ojibwe is an interesting language to study. The words are longer than in English and the grammar is different. By grammar I mean how the words go together so that they make sense.

I was powwow junior princess last year, when Ashley was senior princess. We got to travel to a lot of places — Wisconsin, Toronto, Kettle Point, Chippewa, Muncy. I love traveling. I'd like to go to Mexico, to lots of places and see lots of different cultures.

To become a powwow princess you enter the pageant. You get interviewed, evaluated, you have to dance, you have to know about your culture. You have to walk on a runway and take questions from judges in front of an audience. You have to be able to handle being nervous. If you let your nerves control you, then you won't be able to give good answers and you'll make people think you don't know very much.

Ashley was amazing as powwow princess. She was friendly, beautiful, fun-loving, crazy in a good way. She always made you smile.

She'd tried out for years and never got crowned, and then she finally did, and she was so happy! I know how happy she was because we'd be at the same events and we'd hang out.

A few months ago she killed herself.

It was a big shock to the community.

I don't know why she did it. I had no idea she was going to do it.

Her reign as princess had ended. But that's not a reason to do anything. I couldn't tell what was wrong. She always seemed so smiling and happy.

I heard about teen suicide happening in other First Nations communities. I guess I always thought it happens somewhere else, but not here and not to people I know.

First Nations kids have more challenges than white kids. There's always racism. I hear comments a lot when I'm in town. Even from adults in shops or on the street. Whites think our cultures and beliefs are stupid and that we are worthless. It's hard to keep yourself believing in yourself because the noise coming from the white people is so loud. They assume we're all bad and into drugs and crime. They don't bother to try to get to know us.

Some white adults talk to us really kindly, implying nasty things but using sweet voices, so if you try to call them on it they can pretend to not know what you're talking about.

Maybe it all just wore Ashley down. We'll probably never know.

I don't think I'll enter the senior powwow princess pageant. All my princess memories are with Ashley and I don't think it would feel very good to go on now that she's dead.

I hang out with her brother sometimes. He seems okay, like he forgets about it, but I think he just hides his emotions. Her mom has other kids. She has to keep going.

To other kids who have lost someone, it might help if you write a letter to the person to express your feelings. When you're done, you can keep it in a memory box or you can burn it and watch the smoke rise up to heaven, or you can leave it on their grave. Whatever feels right. In case there are things you didn't say to them while they were alive.

But it's better to tell them in person.

And it's a whole lot better if they don't die.

Hillary, 18

Many Aboriginal women in Canada have been murdered or gone missing, and some research suggests that in the past twenty years, the number of disappearances and homicides may be in the hundreds. Although Aboriginal people make up about 4 percent of the total Canadian population, they make up 27 percent of all homicide victims. According to Statistics Canada, the murder rate for Aboriginal women is seven times higher than the rate for non-Aboriginal victims, and the missing and murdered women have left behind hundreds of motherless children.

Hillary's sister was murdered at the age of fifteen.

I am a mixture of Huron, Cree, Mi'kmaq, Ojibwe and Métis. And Norwegian.

My sister Dolly was murdered a year ago. She was fifteen.

I helped my mother and my older sister pick out her headstone. I wanted it to be something she would like. Sisters know what a sister would want. It looks like an open book and it's got the words In God's Loving Care carved into it along with doves. It was expensive, but it's the last gift we'll ever be able to give her.

She went missing three weeks before they found her body. She was living in Sudbury, the city I live in now. Our mother used to live here too, but she's gone back to Kapuskasing because she finds Sudbury too scary. My father is still in Sudbury. I like being here because my sister is buried here and I wouldn't want to go and leave her alone. It is a scary place though. Drugstores are always being robbed for OxyContin.

It was a terrible three weeks, the weeks she went missing. We couldn't get anyone to take it seriously. It wasn't until she turned up dead that the police got on board.

My mother was going frantic. You can imagine. It's not that Dolly was an angel, but she'd always call. Even at three in the morning she'd call for Mom to pick her up if she was at a friend's house and it wasn't a good scene. Always. And she knew Mom would never be angry at her for calling. She'd always call just to let Mom know where she was and that she was okay. Mom told that to the police. The police ignored her.

"She's just at a friend's house," the police said. "She's a teenager. Maybe she's mad at you."

Later they said, "Oh, she's probably run away to Toronto. She'll call home when she gets tired of the big city." There were other teenaged girls from Sudbury who went missing and turned up as prostitutes in Toronto. I'll bet you anything those girls didn't become prostitutes because they liked having sex with strange men. Someone forced them into it. But that wasn't considered serious by the police, because they were just Native girls.

Same with the media. The same time my sister went missing, a white girl from the south of Ontario went missing, and that was all over the national news. Mom kept going to the local affiliate to get them to cover Dolly's disappearance and nothing happened. She finally threatened to set up a picket line outside the TV station, and then they ran the story locally. The national news never covered my sister's disappearance and death. Ducks nesting in a hotel pond made the national news, but my sister's murder didn't.

We even set up our own search party. Mom asked the cops for advice on how to do it but they never got back to her. We had to just do it as best we could. We went out looking for her a lot in different parts of the city. We looked around this tent city set up along the railway tracks where people aren't supposed to be camping but they have no other homes. We searched parks, towns around Sudbury, wasteland places. I remember searching out in the bush with some friends. It was raining hard and the car got stuck in the mud. We looked in woodpiles, creeks, highway underpasses. Everywhere we could think of.

It turns out she was murdered the same night she went missing. The police found her body in a wooded area by a lake.

They caught the two guys who did it. One is an adult, over the legal age. The other is a young offender. They're white.

I went to one of the bail hearings. Dolly's killer just stared at me, sneering. My boyfriend was with me and stared him down. I heard later that they made jokes about killing her.

The police kept Dolly's body for three weeks until they let us bury her. It came out in court what those men did to her. They crushed and burned her. They're not human. They can't be human. But what else are they, if not human? Mom would like them to tell her why they did it, but I know that there is no why. They just did it.

They didn't get bail. The dad of one of them would have bailed him out, but my mom went to him and said, "You're worried about your son, and you have my sympathies. But my daughter's not coming home. And your son's not coming home any time soon either."

My mom's amazing. She's visually impaired but she's one of those moms that has eyes in the back of her head.

I've heard that the guys are going to plead guilty. Maybe they'll have some explanation then of why they did it. But again, there is no why. There is no way to understand it.

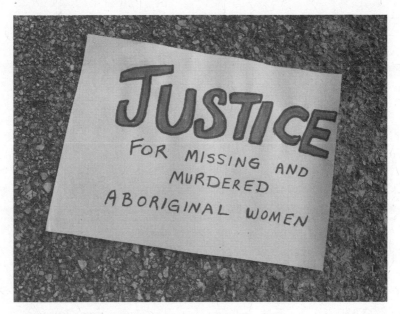

Sign at a memorial vigil.

After they were arrested, a Native guy came up to my mother on the street and said, "Don't worry. The Native Mafia will take care of those guys." The cops say that the Native Mafia is worse than the Italian Mafia because when the Native Mafia do something, they leave no trace.

My boyfriend is in jail right now. He has some addiction struggles. He's in the same facility as one of my sister's killers. The killer was in the visiting room one time when I went in to visit my boyfriend. I complained to the jail officials, but it happened another time. They don't care.

My boyfriend had to really struggle with himself not to hurt this guy. We have a son together. It's important that he get out of jail soon so we can be good parents together. He got himself under control, then asked this guy why he killed Dolly. The guy said for him to tell me he's sorry.

Sorry. He can stick his sorry. How can you apologize for

killing someone? There is no way to apologize for that.

I've since heard about stuff that's happened to both the killers in jail. At first I felt bad for them. They're just young guys. It took me a while to remember that I didn't put them there. They put themselves there. What happens to them is not my fault. When men get hurt, why do women feel guilty? I know what they did, but I don't like the thought of the same thing being done to them.

My boyfriend will get out of jail soon and we'll try to make it work. I dropped out of school. I just couldn't concentrate.

We marked my sister's seventeenth birthday not long ago. I guess we thought it would make us feel better, since we'd be thinking about her anyway. We had a cake and we talked about her.

They say things get easier with time. I just don't know.

Dolly was a terrific fighter. I'm older and bigger but she could whip my ass! She always told me she wouldn't think for a second before trying to hurt some guy who was trying to hurt her. It took two of them to kill her. And she would have made it as hard on them as she could.

How do I raise my son to be a good man? How can I be louder than all the music and all the messages that will tell him that to be a man he must rape and beat women? He's only nine months old now. How can I keep him from becoming the sort of man that would kill a girl like my sister?

Every mother must wonder that. Do fathers worry about that too?

It was lonesome, the leaving.
Husband dead, friends buried
or held prisoner. I felt that I was
leaving all I had but I did not cry.
You know how you feel when you
lose kindred and friends through
sickness. You do not care if you
die. With us it was worse. Strong
men, well women and little children
killed and buried. They had not done
wrong to be so killed. We had only
asked to be left in our own homes,
the homes of our ancestors. Our
going was with heavy hearts, broken
spirits. But we would be free ... All
lost, we walked silently on into the
wintry night.

> — Wetatonmi, widow of Ollokot,
> brother of Chief Joseph of the
> Nez Perce

Zack, 16

First Nations suicide rates are twice as high as the rest of Canada, according to the Aboriginal Healing Foundation. Young people between ten and twenty-nine living on reserves are six times more likely to die of suicide than other youth in the country. Getting help for those in remote communities is difficult, expensive and often not culturally appropriate. Suicide is the second-biggest cause of death for Native American youth.

In response, the Indian Health Service sponsored an Action Summit for Suicide Prevention in 2011. Communities all over North America are looking at what can be done and what is needed to make it happen.

Experts have made a link between Indigenous teen suicides and lack of proper housing, sewers and access to clean water — conditions that can make young people feel that their lives are not valued.

Zack is one young activist who is reaching out to other kids to help save lives.

I'm president of the St. Ignace Tribal Youth Council and part of the Sault Tribe of Chippewa Indians.

Chippewa history is all over the St. Ignace area. It's just across from Mackinac Island. It used to be called Michilimackinac, which is Chippewa for Great Turtle. It looks a bit like a turtle if you look at it in a certain way. But the name got shortened over the years. There's a lighthouse from the 1800s, and colonial Michilimackinac. It's a tourist attraction now, but it was built by the French in 1715, then sacked by the British in the French and Indian War.

The Chippewa didn't like the Brits any better than they liked the French. I'm a descendant of Chief Mackinac, who went to war against the colonials back in the 1700s.

My family has lived on Mackinac Island and around it ever since anyone can remember. Lots of people come here on holiday, especially during the summer, for boating and camping and fishing. It's really beautiful.

But it's a small town, and it's hard to be young and gay in a small town.

I figured out that I was gay when I was in eighth grade. I've always been gay, since I was born, but it took me a while to realize it. I was lucky to realize it when I'm still young. Sometimes people go for almost their whole lives, knowing that something about themselves is different from others but not being able to say what it is. They're so afraid of how others will treat them that they can't even admit it to themselves.

When I came out to my mom, she said, "You're my son. You be a good man and I don't care about anything else."

So that gave me courage, knowing I had my family behind me. And the response from the Native folks I told was — nothing. I was the same person to them that I was before. No difference. That really told me a lot about who we are. I felt very proud.

The white community? Well, that's another story.

I came out to people in the white community when I started my freshman year of high school, and I've been tormented for the last two years. It's been brutal — name calling, harassment, lots of anti-gay and anti-Native stuff. Very ignorant. Very unimaginative.

I can't even walk into school with another kid or they'll get tormented too. So I take care to try to protect the people who are decent to me. It means I'm alone a lot at school.

I spoke to teachers, but they wouldn't back me and wouldn't do anything to stop the bullying. I'd say something to the bullies, and the teachers would write me up for bad behavior. My school operates on a point system. You get so many points and they give you a suspension. I've been suspended a few times for answering back.

But that was last year. I'm heading into the eleventh grade and I'm not worried so much. Words can't hurt me anymore. Plus it's the second-oldest grade in the school. I think I'll be left alone.

Still, I can't wait to get out of here. The town is too small-minded. It's overall too difficult.

But like I said, I'm not too worried. I have a lot of other things to think about.

I'm involved with STAY — Sault Tribe Alive Youth. The goal is to keep our tribal youth alive.

The Sault Lake Chippewa have a suicide rate that's twice the US national average. Twice!

STAY does a lot of presentations to youth groups. We talk not just about suicide but about overall well-being. What do we need to feel well in our spirit, in our bodies? Exercise is a great path to preventing suicide because it makes you feel better and it's good for you. So we organize a lot of long-distance biking for the community. We got more than seventy-five people of all ages out biking with us. We do teen dances, put on a youth empowerment powwow, and do Friends Helping Friends suicide prevention, training ourselves and other kids how to be a good support to someone in trouble. We've reached out to youth who are literally dying to be heard.

I'm president of my local tribal youth council. I started out helping in the community as a youth education assistant. I worked with little kids in the third grade, teaching them things about our culture, showing them how to make dreamcatchers, helping out on camping trips, things like that. As I got older I asked to be part of the tribal youth council.

In our tribal school we put in a Three Sisters Garden — corn, beans and squash. We open up our dances for everyone. We try our best to help the whole community, the white community too. It gets hard to do that when they throw it back in our faces. They do that a lot, making racist comments. It gets me mad. I'm working on learning how to control my anger so that I can still get my point across. Anger is useful only if you use it to get yourself to do something positive.

I lived on the reservation from third grade to seventh grade and then we moved into town. The reservation is three miles out of town. There's a lot of really nice, really great people living there. There's also a big drug problem and drinking, and that can make for a lot of nastiness. It's hard to go out there and see how people are living. People who are addicted need help. Narcotics addicts can be very stubborn. The drug makes them selfish. Makes them think, "I can do what I please and I don't care about anybody else." It's not just Native addicts who think this way. Any addict — white, Asian, whatever. It's a nasty thing.

A lot of white kids come to school in brand new clothes, driving a brand new car. They get everything given to them so nothing has any value. Native kids, we have to work for what we get. My mom had me when she was seventeen and has worked really hard for everything we have. I owe her a lot.

White adults have said to me, "The only thing Indians are good for is getting drunk and dying. Their silly traditions are a waste of time. The whites have the majority. Indians? Who cares?"

They say these things because they lack information. They're just people. We probably have a lot in common. We may even like each other if we got to know each other.

One thing that I think a lot of non-Native people don't understand is that there are so many different tribes and customs and languages. There's not just one Native American community. There's many! All different. People watch bad movies and that's where they get their information from.

I think growing up gay in a small town — and Native gay at that — is really a blessing, even though it's been really difficult at times. It's a blessing because in many ways I'm on the outside of things. This allows me to look in, kind of like through a window, and see things clearly. And it's helped me to have more compassion for others, even for white racists. Something bad must have happened to them for them to behave that way.

I don't know exactly what my future will be. I know I'm going to keep involved in working with Native people. On a personal note, my two big hopes are to travel to Paris and to one day meet Shania Twain.

I had the honor once of being able to listen to a talk by Arnold Thomas. He's with the Shoshone-Paiute Tribe of the Duck Valley. When he was in high school he was really good at sports. All the universities wanted him. Then his dad killed himself. Arnold took it hard. When he turned eighteen he tried to shoot himself in the head, but the rifle slipped. Left his face mangled, left him blind. He couldn't even speak for years. But his community stayed by him. He went on to get a master's degree. And now he helps others who are thinking about suicide.

In his speech he said do not be ashamed of who you are. If you are ashamed or afraid, it could cost you your life. He said to give the people you live with a hug, because they are teaching you how to be, whether they are teaching you good things or bad things, you are learning from them, and then you can go out into the world and decide.

When his talk was over, I went up and asked him how he felt when he realized he had survived the suicide attempt. He said that initially he wished he could turn back the clock and do it right. But then he wondered how far he'd have to turn the clock back. His dad committed suicide, his grandfather committed suicide. He had a lot of time to think while he was in the hospital.

Then he told me we are a powerful, strong people. They tried really hard to kill us all off, and we're still here!

I guess that sums up my philosophy too. I'm hopeful about the future of Native Americans. I've been able to meet Native youth from all over, and I've seen first hand what we can do, and what people did for us before we came along.

We're going to keep moving forward.

Arnold W. Thomas can be reached at www.whitebuffaloknife.com

McCayla, 12

Powwows keep traditional Indigenous practices alive and share culture with others. For families that have been torn apart by violence, addictions, residential schools or adoption, powwows can help people to find their way back to their home.

Powwows can be found all over North America, and people of all cultures are welcome to attend in respect and celebration.

I met McCayla at the Black River Pow Wow in Wadhams, Michigan.

I'm Ojibwe, and going into the seventh grade in the fall.

This is my third year at this powwow.

All the regalia has a meaning and comes from a tradition. The feathers are sacred. The fans are to worship the Creator. And the ribbons — when you move, the ribbons flow like the wind.

My grandmother made my dress. I think it's beautiful and I love wearing it.

It didn't take me long to learn how to dance. I wasn't formally taught, like in a school. I watched the older girls and tried to copy them. When I get more used to it I'll put my own little spin on it. I'll bring a bit of myself to the dance.

I practice a lot during the school year, although not in

school. I wish I could study this stuff in school. It's as important as all the other history we learn, and way more important to me than studying wars and explorers.

There was a Native cultural class outside of school for a while. I loved going to that. They taught us drumming, what the regalia means, how to make parts for our own regalia, how to speak our language. I know how to count to ten in the Ojibwe language and how to sing some of the songs. English is my first language, but it's a new language for us, a foreign language. When I speak my own language, it's like I'm talking to my ancestors. It's hard to explain, but it's important, and it makes me feel important.

I'm a Fancy dancer. I wear a shawl draped across my shoulders and when I open it up it looks like a butterfly. When I dance it's like I'm coming out of a cocoon.

If you want to dance at a powwow, you're the one who chooses the kind of dance you want to do. But if you want to be a Jingle dancer, you have to earn the jingles with good behavior or good deeds. There are 365 jingles on the Jingle Dance dress. They can be taken away too. An elder is the one who decides. I'm hoping to be a Jingle Dance dancer when I'm a little older.

The grand entry at a powwow is really special. Everyone comes in and the audience stands out of respect. No one is supposed to take photos during the grand entry because it's a sacred time, but a lot of the white people who come don't bother to read the brochure and they take their cameras out like they're bird-watching. It used to really annoy me. Now I just concentrate on the drums and the dance and ignore them.

I want white people to come to our powwows because they'll learn more about our culture. When they don't know, they do stupid things, like say, "Watch out. That Indian will scalp you!" and other stuff. They don't know any better so you have to forgive them. That's what I was taught.

The powwow dancing takes place in a circle representing the earth. The elders enter first and you always enter and leave the circle from the same spot. And you always travel in the same direction. You always travel clockwise.

My family has always been from this area, at least as far as I know. I'm here with my mother and grandmother.

My grandmother was taken away from her birth family when she was really small and raised by white people. They didn't tell her she was Native. They raised her to believe she was of French and Irish descent. It wasn't until about twelve years ago, when she connected with some members of her birth family, that she found out she was Ojibwe.

She says it was a shock. When she was growing up, to be Native was something to be ashamed of. Native people were not allowed to be proud like we are today. People who were Native were thought by whites to have less value even than people who were Black. And if you know American history, you know that's pretty low!

But Gran also says that as soon as she heard she was Ojibwe, it felt right. It felt like a piece of her that had always been out of place fell into place and she felt like a whole person for the first time in her life. She met her birth aunt and that felt like her real family.

Being Native back then meant that white people thought you were dirty, and if you could hide it, if your skin was white enough, then you kept it secret, under wraps, and didn't discuss it. Otherwise, it would not be good.

I don't know why my people have been treated so badly. We founded this country, but instead of learning from us and thanking us, which would have been smart and polite, white people killed us.

White people still sometimes think that Indians are just like in the movies — movies made by white people! But, like I said, they don't know any better so I have to forgive them.

I have family in Michigan and family in Canada, around Sarnia. There didn't used to be a border. My ancestors would just go from one place to another, no gates or guards. It was all their land.

In school, math and English language arts are my best subjects. I've just started in the band. I'm learning clarinet. Social studies is not so good. It depends on the teacher whether it's interesting or not. In sixth grade we studied the United States, Mexico, the West Indies and South America. In seventh grade we're going to learn about China and Europe.

The other kids at my school know I'm Ojibwe and they find it interesting. They don't make fun of me or say stupid things, but if they did, it would just make them look stupid. It wouldn't touch me. But they don't give me a hard time. I'm one of the top students and I try to be friendly with everybody. You never know who's going to turn out to be a really good friend!

My hair is short right now but it used to be really long. I donated it this past spring to make wigs for kids who have cancer or who have lost their hair for some other reason. It's the second time I've done it. It takes eighteen ponytails of the same shade to make just one wig! I figure, I have hair, so others should have hair too. I don't care if my hair goes to a Native kid or a white kid. It really doesn't matter. After all, we're all human beings.

Waasekom, 17

In Ojibwe and other Indigenous traditions, there are Seven Sacred Teachings, handed down through the generations. It is said that following these teachings or values is the road to an honorable life.

The Seven Teachings are Wisdom, Love, Truth, Courage, Honesty, Humility and Respect.

Waasekom tries to live by these teachings.

I am an Ojibwe from the Saugeen First Nation. My spirit name is Waasekom.

When we speak to the spirits we speak in Ojibwe because the spirits don't understand English. You need to know who you are in your own language.

My spirit name means when it's night and lightning fills the sky and it suddenly looks like daylight.

Every day I get up and put on a mask to protect myself before I go out into the world. It's the way I survive. There are a lot of ignorant people out there. It's hard to be around them. They can wound your spirit if you're not careful.

Even when people try not to be ignorant, there are many things that infect their minds to keep them from being free. Some kids get all excited about a new video game and never consider that they're buying into a system that will hijack their minds.

One of my relatives was murdered by the police. His name was Dudley George.

There's a strip of land along Lake Huron that used to belong to First Nations people. It got stolen by the government, of course, and a military base got put on it. "We'll give it back to you at the end of the war," the government told us, but they didn't, of course. They turned it into a provincial park. We got tired of waiting, so Dudley and some others took over the park and declared it Indian land.

The government probably thought it would be good for votes if they went after the Indians so they sent in the police. There was a standoff for a while. Then the police said Dudley was coming at them with a gun, so they shot him a bunch of times and killed him.

Except there was no gun. Everyone knew no one in the park had a gun. Only the police had guns. Even the police knew the Indians had no guns. But they kept lying about it and lying about it, until finally they were forced to tell the truth.

Sam George, Dudley's brother, forced them to tell the truth. He put up a hard fight but then he died. So they're both dead.

There has to be a better way of doing things.

People should just let other people be. The people in the government who make decisions for us have no idea who First Nations people really are. They have no clue. They lump us all in together. They think we're all the same.

It's an up-and-down relationship I have with myself. It's a fight to remember who I am and to stay true to who I am. The world doesn't make it easy. There's so much noise everywhere. It's hard to find a quiet place and time to sort myself out.

When I get older I don't want to just succumb to not saying anything about injustice because that's the easier road to
go down. I want to fight for what's right. If you don't fight
for that, you're already dead. You might be walking around
but you're dead inside.

When I experience reality for what it is and not just for
what I want it to be, it stains, but it's liberating too.

We are a disabled people because of what's been done to
us through history, but we can rehabilitate ourselves. But we
have to face the truth, all of us, before we can move forward.
Kids get lied to all the time in school. They know it but they
get used to it. They begin to believe that the lies are as good
as it gets.

It's better when we can see ourselves and each other with
clear eyes and open hearts.

I'm spending more time these days learning about my culture. I contemplate on the medicine wheel, thinking about
traditional teachings. I help out with teaching the Ojibwe
language to little kids so that they have the sounds of the
ancestors in their heads. Then when the ancestors speak to
them, they'll be able to understand.

There are two sides to life. One is the deeper, spiritual
side. The other is having to pay bills and deal with the white
world. In that world I will need skills so that I can earn money and take care of business. I'm a good student. There's a lot
I could do. The trick is to keep from getting too pulled into
the world of money.

I do my best to follow the Seven Sacred Teachings. In
my quiet time I think about them, about what I'm learning
and where my weaknesses are, and I pray for guidance and
strength.

Seeing the work that Sam George did inspires me a lot.

He wanted to know why his brother was killed. And he kept going until he had an answer.

My gran was one of the community members who stood with Dudley and the others. A lot of brave people had a role in that occupation, getting in food, taking care of children, keeping the people warm and calm.

Gran raised so many kids, not just her own. She'd come around in her van, honk the horn and all us kids would pile in. She didn't have money to do anything with us, but we all wanted to be around her because she had such life inside her. Jesus Christ was probably a lot like my grandma.

I speak a lot at rallies and events because I've learned to control and channel my anger. When I speak, I speak with authority, yet people can see that I'm a peaceful person. I've worked hard to get this way and I still have a long way to go. I'm not like most guys my age who waste their time listening to the sort of music that poisons their mind.

I need my mind clear and strong. There's work to be done.

Each of us is put here in this time
and in this place to personally
decide the future of humankind.
Do you think you were put here for
something less?
— Chief Arvol Looking Horse

RESOURCES

There are many wonderful organizations that provide a wealth of information about Indigenous people. This is only a partial list.

Activism

The American Indian Movement (www.aimovement.org) is a civil rights activist organization founded in 1968 to encourage self-determination among Native peoples and to establish international recognition of their treaty rights.

The Indigenous Environmental Network (www.ienearth.org) works to protect Indigenous lands and to assert the sovereignty and jurisdictional rights of Indigenous nations.

Addictions

White Bison (www.whitebison.org) offers sobriety, recovery, addictions prevention and wellness/Wellbriety learning resources to the Native American community

Children and Youth

The Creating Hope Society (www.creatinghopesociety.ca) regularly holds a Blanket of Remembrance Round Dance to honor children who have died in foster care.

The National Indian Child Welfare Association/NICWA (www.nicwa .org) is a national voice for American Indian children and families. The organization focuses on the tribal capacity to prevent child abuse and neglect.

The National Indian Youth Council/NIYC (www.niyc-alb.org) has thousands of members worldwide and works to ensure that every Native American has an equal opportunity to excel and become a viable member of his/her community.

United National Indian Tribal Youth/UNITY (www.unityinc.org) operates 150 councils in the United States and Canada.

Community

The National Association of Friendship Centres (nafc.ca) provides programs and services for Aboriginal people in Canadian cities, especially those making the transition from rural, remote and reserve life to an urban environment.

Conservation

Southwest Conservation Corps (sccorps.org) is a non-profit agency that provides young men and women with service and educational opportunities through projects that promote personal growth, the development of social skills and an ethic of natural resource stewardship.

Culture

Every year more than three thousand Indigenous dancers and singers representing more than five hundred tribes from Canada and the US go to Albuquerque, New Mexico, to participate at the Gathering of Nations Powwow (www.gatheringofnations.com). For more information about powwows and Native American people and cultures, and to find out when and where powwows are held across North America, to go www.powwows.com.

The Indian Pueblo Cultural Center (www.indianpueblo.org) preserves and advances the accomplishments and evolving history of the Pueblo people of New Mexico.

The Inuit Broadcasting Corporation (www.inuitbroadcasting.ca) provides a window to the Arctic by producing television programming by Inuit and for Inuit. Tungasuvvingat Inuit (www.tungasuvvingatinuit.ca) provides Inuit-specific programs, services and support to empower and enhance the lives of Inuit.

For the past ninety years, the Santa Fe Indian Market (www.swaia.org) has brought together gifted Native American artists and visitors and collectors from around the world. It is the largest Native American arts show and New Mexico's largest annual weekend event, drawing 150,000 visitors each year.

Six Nations Indian Museum (www.sixnationsindianmuseum.com) provides education about Native American history in general and Haudenosaunee culture in particular, including information about the Land Ethic of the Haudenosaunee and other environmental sensibilities.

Woodland Cultural Centre (www.woodland-centre.on.ca) is a nonprofit organization that preserves and promotes the culture and heritage of the First Nations of the Eastern Woodland area.

Education

The American Indian College Fund (www.collegefund.org) provides Native students with scholarships and provides financial support for the country's 34 accredited tribal colleges and universities.

The Martin Aboriginal Education Initiative (www.maei-ieam.ca) aims to improve elementary and secondary school education for Aboriginal Canadians.

Gangs

For information on how to get out of a gang, go to Gang Prevention (www.gangprevention.ca) or Gang Rescue and Support Project/ GRASP (www.graspyouth.org), a peer-run intervention program that works with youth who are at risk of gang involvement or who are in gangs, as well as helping families of gang victims.

Residential Schools

The Aboriginal Healing Foundation (www.ahf.ca) seeks to support all those who have been affected by the legacy of the physical, sexual, mental, cultural and spiritual abuses of the Indian residential schools.

Indian Residential Schools Survivor's Society (www.irsss.ca) assists First Peoples in British Columbia to recognize and support those affected by residential schools.

The Legacy of Hope Foundation (www.legacyofhope.ca) is a Canadian charitable organization aimed at raising awareness and understanding of the legacy of residential schools, including the effects and intergenerational impacts on First Nations, Métis and Inuit peoples, and to support the ongoing healing of residential school survivors.

The Truth and Reconciliation Commission of Canada (www.trc.ca) has a mandate to learn the truth about what happened in the residential schools and to inform all Canadians about this.

Sports

The Canadian Lacrosse Hall of Fame (www.canadianlacrossehalloffame.org) includes a museum and archives located in New Westminster, British Columbia. In the United States, US Lacrosse (www.uslacrosse.org) provides programs and services to inspire participation in lacrosse and protect the integrity of the sport.

All Nations Skate Jam (allnationsskatejam.com) is a skateboard-centered outreach program that provides safe and healthy recreational activities and lifestyle choices to Native youth.

Suicide Prevention

Honouring Life Network (www.honouringlife.ca) offers culturally relevant information and resources to help Aboriginal youth and youth workers dealing with suicide profession.

The National Suicide Prevention Lifeline (www.youmatter.suicidepreventionlifeline.org) provides help for young people who are struggling, as well as for their family members and friends.

Sault Tribe Alive Youth/STAY (www.stayproject.org) contains good information and resources for teens on suicide prevention, bullying prevention and other issues.

Women

The Amnesty International report, "No More Stolen Sisters" (www .amnesty.ca/our-work/issues/indigenous-peoples/no-more-stolen -sisters) calls for a stop to violence against First Nations, Inuit and Métis women. "Maze of Injustice: The Failure to Protect Indigenous Women from Violence" (www.amnesty.org/en/library/info/ AMR51/035/2007) focuses on sexual violence against Native American women.

The Native American Women's Health Education Resource Center/ NAWHERC (www.nativeshop.org) has become the leading American pathfinder in addressing Indigenous women's reproductive health and justice issues while working to preserve and protect Native American culture.

The Native Women's Association of Canada/NWAC (www.nwac.ca) works with organizations such as the United Nations and Amnesty International to advance the well-being of Aboriginal women and girls, as well as their families and communities.

Deborah Ellis is best known for her Breadwinner series, set in Afghanistan and Pakistan — a series that has been published in twenty-five languages, with more than one million dollars in royalties donated to Canadian Women for Women in Afghanistan and Street Kids International. She has won the Governor General's Award, the Ruth Schwartz Award, the University of California's Middle East Book Award, Sweden's Peter Pan Prize, the Jane Addams Children's Book Award and the Vicky Metcalf Award for a Body of Work. She has received the Ontario Library Association's President's Award for Exceptional Achievement, and she has been named to the Order of Ontario.

Deborah lives in Simcoe, Ontario.

Loriene Roy, Ph.D., is Anishinabe, enrolled on the White Earth Reservation, a member of the Minnesota Chippewa Tribe. A former president of the American Library Association, she is a professor at the University of Texas at Austin. She is the founder and director of "If I Can Read, I Can Do Anything," a national reading club for American Indian Students.